Steven Duplij

SUPERMANIFOLD OF LIFE

Multilingual poems and short prose

TRILINGUAL PRESS
Cambridge, Massachusetts, USA
2014

Supermanifold of Life

Poems and short prose in English, French, German, Italian, Norwegian, Polish, Portuguese, Serbian and Spanish

Author: Steven Duplij (Stepan Douplii, Степан Дуплий)
Design: Mariya Antyufeyeva (Мария Антюфеева)
Translators: Caroline Aeby, Pedro Alvarez, Chris Bernard, Iver Brevik,
             Paul Cariage, Roberto Casalbuoni, Christine Clairmont,
             Branko Dragovich, Steven Duplij, Marian Jaskula,
             Trudi Kiebala, Volker Knecht, Miguel Krshjschanows,
             Grzegorz Kwiatkowski, Peter Mahnke, V. Morillon, Edda and
             Wolfram Von Oertzen, Terezinka Pereira

TRILINGUAL PRESS
PO Box 391206
Cambridge, MA 02139
USA

trilingualpress@tanbou.com

ISBN-10: 1-9364-3108-4 Trilingual Press
ISBN-13: 978-1-936431-08-3 Trilingual Press

Contents

Poems in English

Translated by Steven Duplij

POEPHYSICS

Poetry, a supernova of feelings. Physics, a supernova of ideas. A new string of letters, a new string of mathematical symbols are the two sides of the Moon, an alien binary. Behind my soul they form a sphinx. I do not put apart the ideas of Physics and the metaphors of Poetry. The uncontrollable cold–fusion is necessary for my heart to create them. The newer the fuel is the farther the shot into the Future will be.

I believe Poetry cannot be constructed as a formula. Outer rules are transparent for Her, and only inner ones alive. The only rule is true: without a critical mass the reaction of Creativity will not start. Feelings and ideas are collapsed to the densities so large that independently of my desire there is an explosion into Infinity.

They are all–penetrating. Simply I am not able to avoid them, and I am not afraid any more that somebody will be grinning over my weakness, my sufferings, my complexes, my minuses.

Poephysics lets me elevate myself over them, over the way of life, over Time.

NEXT FAKE YEAR

The year – gone,
The life – dismissed.
I cry – begone!
The answer – "blissed".

I need – to be,
But fate – as is,
As biting bee
Perverting kiss.

Call-back is dead,
All colors – grey.
Desires – spread,
All friends – away.

They love – for sale,
Become turnstile.
I carry sail:
Last shot – a smile.

The country – lies:
`All things must pass'.
The freedom – dies,
Fake future – grass...

PLANE

You have yours, I have mine
We can wait for our souls' sunshine

Do you forget, remember? – No?
Press 'Enter' button after 'Hope'

Future awaits – make no mistake
Let's explore true feelings lake

Common dream's plane is taking off
Inner constraints and the past – below

You have yours, I have mine
Can we wait for our souls' sunshine?..

WINDOW

Awakening... her alien bed...
I'm sick and drunk,
And full of mad
Emotions, feelings
Memories...

My Lord! Forgive me –
Set me free
From ugly loneliness
And stone
Of bared reproach less
Than moan.

I saw Trance Window
To the dark –
Its wind was burying
Last soul's mark...

ALIEN

I'm not a stranger –
I am – a man,
Love – inner changes,
Have – what I can.

I'm not an alien
Among memories –
Searching for spelling
Of supreme tries.

Twisting the spaces
Of different lies,
I melt in traces
Of pain – not to die...

A VERY "HAPPY" NEW YEAR

City – is dead,
People – are drunk.
Soul – is sad,
Life – was a junk.

Rain lost His tears,
Brain lost its mind.
Empty frontiers
Out of line.

Heart – as in false,
Goal – as in wrong.
Deep sense – in nulls:
God says: "Begone!"...

INSTEAD

Instead of her
I melt in them –
My love and word,
And soul's anthem.
Instead of my
Having lived life out –
Nobody shines
From ashes' crowd.
Instead of song –
I cry the End
And pray: "so long"
My inside's land.
Instead of death –
I wait more roles
To play the best
Without goals.

WEBGIRL

She came to me from Web –
I know you.
She told to understand –
Believe in you.

She smiled at my naiveness –
Forgive you.
To hope fulfil the last guess –
I wait for you.

Kill their under feelings –
Forget them.
We are each others foundlings –
Of last item.

I know what is loneliness –
You knew the Tool.
Please throw away your pastness –
I'll too.

We open door out nothingness –
To live
For singing souls crying rest –
Motif.

US AND THEM

My love, your love
Considered as continuations
Have been, by now, killed.
By whom? –
By us
And them.
I'm gnawed, you're gnawed
By loneliness and inspiration
Of our torn up feelings.
By whom? –
By them
And us.
We try to laugh,
To salute Freedom Station
Which's melting into the crying mirage.
Whose guilt? –
Of us
And them.
We thought enough
To close pagination
Of our senseless story-building.
For whom? –
For them
And us.

HATE

Do hate your Fate
For losing door
Into disgrace
To wish no more.
Do lay on grave
Of lying smile
Without stay
To close survival.

Do try to fight
With inner sins,
Forgetting light
From wrong way things.

Do feel hot steel
Of coming guns
Perverting bill
Do make your brain
Be free from null,
Do sit in train
Of yelling Rule.

Forgive me reef
Of wasting goals –
My last belief
Became a role.

FILE

Me not to strive to open file
      of new relations,
Wall white: you, Loneliness,
Screen's points – empty imitations.

They say the same, they love as if
      their drink turned beer,
My bare and hard inside for them is
      only function mere.

I'm praying: bill me, God, I'll pay
      my soul's arrears
Before your long-awaited word-appeal
      makes me disappear.

Last plot of the inevitable downfall
      burns low,
My dreams were perfectly betrayed
      and shot.
        I go...

DREAM

I dreamt of night –
The garden of graves.
Two steps – away
Go the debts of my soul.
The nimbus melted   I pray: do read
Extorting a moan.   A moment yelling,
Stand still   Do not dare leave
Life-cyclotron!   Concealing your face.
Please flood with Dream
The stagnated Meaning
To burn to ashes
For Fate's encore.
Forgive my wrecking
And failures, soul selling.
There's is the delirium –
Mine is Work, Home, Morgue.
I've stonily awoken –
A ray is gliding
Off the bottom of madness:
I'll keep the coup inside me.
Naivete gnaws, hurts, revenges.
My Sin is dethroned – the fancy-realm AIDS.

HEAR ME

I am full of prayer
Chalice has been thrown away.
My liberation
Is out of trouble.
The breath of a straw
Mowed down
Has gotten cold.
Begone!
Futility of hatred
Which has been fed up.
The end of Dream –
Under-paintedness of the past
Chastity canvas:
Please, hear me.
O! Lord!
Please, hear me,
Please, hear...

DIVORCE

Yelling I'll be divorced with myself –
Not for the sake for the drama.
I'll over-yearn for the footprint
Which is rotted through by Fate.
My supermoan has been deceived
By the strange meaning
Of the inviolable pseudo years.
Stand up!
Do not waste yourself
For the Nothingness.
Do not build in my heart the cathedral
Diseased with the infidelity leucosis.
I'll burn prognoses by the Star
Calling into the Night.
I'll stick together the roses
With my guiltiness.
I'm finding my daughter
In one of them,
In others...
My naivete – begone!

DIVINE BEVERAGE

The world of illusions
Is the divine beverage.
The indispensability of the courage
Will absorb their aimlessness.
Only by the beaten gladness
And the hatred of evil
You cannot multiply
Their modulus of rage
With the shamed maimedness.
Stand still!
The stiff gelatine
Of the non-time.
Please, squeeze Dream
In the grip of despair
And dwindle
The nilpotent quagmire
Of the non-space!
Though I have not known
The salty smell of the Sun:
Do not hide your face!
Please, give up yourself
To the other march,
To the spat fancy realm.

MELTING

Melting in the Naivete's pores
Of my yelling and stretched soul
Being swaddled by questions,
Arguing with Heaven,
The relaxation of doubts
Are drugging me to infinite dreams' precipice –
Please, write!
Painting the night of meanings
In a hundred of fresh and morbid flowers
Becoming covered with vileness,
I am holding my exaltation
On the manege
Of my helical pseudo-life
Sewn in a slapdash manner
From the bits of Dream.
Making advances to the Fancy Realm's lash
By the outer and tired
From its insincerity ditch
Of the marks warped with Depth,
I am praising the same Face,
I am having a foreboding about the scrap.
The cruelty of lying-prophets' rules
Will keep back the pouring of itself
Into the abyss of them –
But only for a moment.
The thought will freeze with hope
That this is not the last,
The last of my verses...

CURTAIN

No!
I haven't gone away –
I only hate
The Past,
I'm irritated
Devilishly
That I'm alive.
It's reckless inadvertence
Of loving bitter enemies.
I've seen growing faint –
I have been tired.
I have found Life
As if for fun.
But where is it,
Where is, on earth, meaning
And the heart-rending Call
Saving me
From the infinite fall.
The last hall –
Is the illusions' ball.
And the curtain has fallen....

FACE

I see the grinning Face
In reddish light again,
I sing the final song
And cry: Begone!

My losses wait
And try to hate
All my false pasts
To choose the last.

I see the Stop
And call the Hope,
But His reply
Is short: You die.

BONE OF TIME

The bone of Time
Is drawing the piles
Of Events
Into the soul's depth,
Without noticing
That I'm still alive.
Let the footprint
Of desire melt
Into the ashes of disbelief –
Do not do that –
I belong to you.
But I'm in love
In loneliness somewhat –
Do not waste
Your jealously in vain –
Create yourself
And us.
Let Lie
Full gallop and away
Into worn out spume.
Love – is
Like Eternal Time.
The last spectator-player,
Laughing,
Is climbing up
The asymptotic stage
Of Life
To be melted into the Nite...

BRAND

I'm not putting a brand on them
Leaving into space –
There is no place.
Their scalpel made by life
Is tenderly kissing.
I'm hoping,
Burning down,
I'm wearing myself –
And sleeping.
Yes!
These have long ago disappeared,
There is the hearty laughter,
Splash:
The etheric wind of Time
Is silent,
And the diffidence of Dream
Is angering,
And the Grief
Is consuming.

FREEZING

Freezing in the night, my gibberish
Has got free with a dream
By the silence unrestrained.
Oh, you! The infinite ball
Of the downcast promises,
Burning the jungles of years,
Do abate!
The last accord has been sung –
The soul over-yells the moan,
Which is round the throat necklace
Of the meeting with another soul.

Riddling with the kisses,
The vicious stage of Hope –
Do burn out!
The stupor
Howl
Of wind –
The grown stiff
Layer of ash
I'll take,
Contract –
I'll go pass
To my eternal rest...

HOLDING MYSELF

I live in vain
To speak of gain
About pain
Of my dead brain.

I love meanwhile
The closed file
Of wasteful life
To miss its knife.

I carry stone –
Eternal moan
Of mine, alone,
To hold my own...

SIEVE

Turning over pages of streets split
Of alien cities' warped bodies,
I asked the Shadow over them swirling
Whence execution of dreams comes.

Meaning bespattered
                              cuts off the meeting
With blows of beggars
                              and lashes of gods:
Next the flight – sieve of partings
Sifts the remainder
                    of nonsensical words.

I smooth design of transmuting to
                                   tenderness
With hackneyed gestures
                              of mannered days
Not living on negligence
                              of empty non-texts
For a long time,
              which is harsher than death.

INFINITE ATONEMENT

In that World,
Like on edge of a blade,
I'm catching at air of Soul.
Smiling, I've been reared by losses.
What remained for myself? – To write.

What to write, when the sticky Time
Is cognized after its disappearance.
Abandoned by them on off-chance
My reflection – skeleton withered.

I'm making my bed for two
For them not to appear from There.
Till the morning I save my warmth
Why, be neither these nor those.

At that time, going mad with fear,
With Infinity I mottle my paper.
Maybe, this is their atonement:
I drink up everything getting cold
On the Bottom.

In that World,
Like on the edge of a blade...

ANGEL

Do not be sad, my Evil's Angel:
Not everything has passed –
               the moan, passion.
My tired soul was embracing
With yearning on the injured
                  graveyard.

Do not raise bridges on the vault
Of all absorbing bondages –
The wasted of shoots and nonsense
Of years lost and useless words.

Do make them pray for happiness,
Do not defame yourself in filth.
The Fate has closed verdict lying
Upon my wrists and scoffs again.

And – rendezvous with motif crazy
Is ceasing. Knocking at the Night,
Excreting cluster of excuses,
Naive, I'll take the rule of them.

INCORRECT DREAM

Next morning I see
>>the incorrect dream:
I am in the Past, fall in love,
>>>>dearest – alive.
Torturing odour of hands ungentle,
The feast of habitual vices.
>>>Knock – suddenly:
She came without permission.
>>>>>Sobbing.
The Fate yelling prayed –
>>>as one ought. Fever.
The branches of terrible Hope rot
>>>>behind the window
Split with abyss of losses,
>>>I accept demolition,
But only as playing from above,
>>>>>laughing
Converting the maiden-pain
>>>>into my line.
Next morning I see
>>the incorrect dream:
I am in the Past, fall in love,
>>>>dearest – alive...

PASTNESS

Leaves – are covered
With other ones.
Lives – are melted
Over them.
Reflection – stop!
I am alive.
Leaves – are covered
With other ones.

Tenderness – takes over
Its parting.
Sinfulness – overcomes
Rejoicing.
To be shot by moment –
Conceal your lot.
Tenderness – takes over
Its parting.

Pastness – gives up
Way today.
Sickness –
Of unfinished tables.
World perverted in laugh –
Hypocritical they.
Pastness – gives up
Way today.

ICON

Transparent eyes,
Affected tears
Call to the soul's bottom
Stronger than Fate.
And nothing more to say –
Metamorphoses burn me
Embroidering the summons
To wash away the Slave.
The obstinacy of Nought,
The distances are blind...
Caressing flowers perished
With foam of the dreams.
I put on leaves of bliss,
I colour lying scaffold
In the primordial trace
To harden like a madman.
Disfiguring Motif
I glue up moan with verses,
Insatiable words.
I grasp with the pain of years
For roses' strongest wish.
I have been rotten, staying
Alive as a Skeleton
Of debts to have been gnawed
And have already gone.
Surmounting the Night
I come to open space,
To set for them the Candle

Adhered to the hand.
The Icon. They: my son
And daughter – stolen by way of life,
Landscape, some trees, and Light...

PASSENGER

I am only a funny passenger
Of the train passing Nowhere,
Halts of cold apartments
And fruitless searches
                have exhausted me.

Forgotten, amusing, anxious
I don't heat the window with breath.
No end for annoying tiring roadsides –
It's bottom of the unavoidable.

Sleeping Earth – is patient cemetery
Threatening with axe-crosses,
Sharp-clawed evil's lightning-paws
Crush my soul into futile cryings.

Hopes are leaven
              for the moment's wind,
Already nobody caresses my pain,
In my eyes as behind shutters white,
There's endless anguish of life.

SEMI

Semitruth and semiconscience,
Semiargument and semilife.
Semiworld? – Is not worth Fate.
Semimemory? – Begone! – I forgot.

Like the purge for souls,
«Semi-» melts the circle of meaning –
With the semireproach a semifoe
Is lying that he is a semifriend.

The sale with semifeelings,
Food is semifinished.
Semihusband-semibrother
Is semifull up with semilove.

Semipower is semifreedom,
All are ashamed
        and make no complaint.
Becoming semi-nations,
We're semisleeping –
           backwards again?

41

VOLUME

I thought in vain –
The time is mine, no hurry.
A foolish dream –
My volume's full of life.
I am becoming mute
Embracing handful pages last
Unread and having mark:
To say for later.

All wasteful surges
Lot will overtake,
That is expounded
In alien volume-walls,
Which are rotten
With oblivion of Inside
Rewarping lying dreams' refrain.

I will approach Him
And smile from the pain, succumbing,
Expecting final words
In brutal feast of the ideas empty
And poisoned gods...

BLITZ

Beyond blinds of my youth – my years
Remelt the Nothingness
With fylfot cross of blisses to brighten
The total with creation famine.

The light on the lines painted
Is frosting with the aching act again
Of «Do forgive me» play –
To others – parts I'll hand.

The dream of Past is spreading
Behind my guilty windows –
I'll stand on Edge to slam them:
A step – and the fly is prejudged.

The closed despondency torus
Is rolling the Fate downwards.
Confession is sprinkling with silence,
With files of my years crushed.

No, I don't fall to my knees,
I do not spill the motif.
Last gamble with my life as if blitz,
Modulation of figures mort.

NUCLEUS

The creeping evening –
            I am tired of years,
Shift moan-gaze
      from the wallpaper to the wreath
Of blisses lost.
My dream decayed as nucleus
Primordial from futile rows of mine.

There are no events –
            I carry the temptations
To their grave:
My soul – sobs violently and my hands
                – in blood.
I leaf through Night. And her miasmas
Stole into my inside
      to rot to shame my strivings dead.
Being fatted with success,
           Naivety slept,
Breaking prognoses
      with the memory of wasted days:
The Fly has stiffen
         on the highest point, laughing
At pseudo-meaning of the formers
           to fall down more painfully.

QUITTING

I've quit living –
What to rush about
On circles clutching with the Bottom
To whitewash Motive,
To shoot at former self –
What happens then?
I have begun
To burn my path' return
By other people, other goals.
Tornado freezing
Of my crucified soul
Connects two faces of the Host.
I've drunk up laughter
By which before
I fed my sickness, breaking
Secretly from them.
I slide towards the Hope
With mouth disfigured by offence.
I've quit living – no answers
To forest of reproaches, reasons.
I've quit living –
Being caught by the Eternal:
My final bar,
My needless verse –
I'm singing still alone...

SUPERMANIFOLD

Doom is covered
       with the snow of idylls –
Whether to save my Light
Or to clothe up
My latest and inner worries
In the mud of the etceteras? No!
Fylfot cross of dreams
Unspoken and not uttered,
Caresses – poisoned by the mind.
Life's supermanifold
Lies
In gibberish...

BETRAYAL NIGHT

Opened into the Infinity Night –
The Earth has grown quiet
For the betrayal of the yesterday.
All perishable thoughts
And painful scenes –
Still linger here.

The dawn is far away –
There remained
So many rubber minutes
To be counted...
The drops of rain
Are hitting the windows...
The soul's fatigue...

CRYING

Crying. I stand by the window –
Everywhere there is
        that cruel silence of mine.
Cri de coeur melts into the night,
Extorting my daughter-hope.

Time revenges for my lying role –
I know it in my heart, but how
        to burn my failures?
The phone has been done to death –
With my dearest
        I've become a widower.

Do not beat me with the past,
        I'm kissing the ground.
What on earth shall I do?
          Get cool for good?
The gibberish glides to the depths
        of my soul.
How not to waste? –
        Write to write yourself out...

EVERYBODY

Pitch darkness – withered candles
Overshadow, from gibberish, plot,
Strange volumes.
Farewell meets
Tear to quanta the dawn
Of seized feelings
Filling with meaning
Prejudging of followed dreams.
Rushing to truth,
I'm being pierced with thought:
In the end everybody betrays.

PHEOPHANIA'S RAIN

Pheophania's rain –
I am freezing from the snow
Of cooling years
Torn away by the Past.
With what to surmount
Their terrible Meaning
Without desertion
From the wearing blisses
Of Naivety's backbitings.

I'm opening the Dreams' Bin
To endure anew
The Bottom's theme hackneyed,
Slipping into the Moan.
How to learn without wasting
That I'm ready without falsehood
For insatiability of Bonds? –
Smell is caressing the Vow.

Pheophania's rain –
There's the infinite beach
Of Hope tired sleeping
And the words unuttered.
Pheophania's rain –
Depth cannot be surveyed
With the emptiness of your previous
And hollow-cheeked Debts.

WREATH

I lay the wreath of guilt
     on the Pseudopast,
I transpose their portraits – into night.
Paint despondency splash
      into impossibility
To transform casual strangers –
      into Daughter.
They are sorrowfully crying
     for mundane losses,
Joys, caresses and lying dreams.
Disturbed by pain of debts
I'm so tired measuring spiral's coils.

Do not cut the thread of the holy frontier
       to Eternity,
Call of Nothing outstrips in fervour
Of the goals unachieved: unconcern
Of impending words,
   in which I already was tormented.
Stepping aside
  from Passion's mirror up to gunfire,
Calming sincerity
     with exploded ashes,
I hide abandonment
   as a first thought
That the marriage
   with my shuttle Fate has been broken.

FLYING

No, it's impossible to drive them out –
And why rush about them?
I'll never pacify
Remains of my shameless conscience.

I shan't forgive myself the treason,
But who can define it?
We're proving by yelling furiously
That we have the right to be like this.

While justifying the every step
We're caressing ourselves
                without doubts,
But we have no better blessings
Besides the lust and laziness.

Goodbye to all,
        may peace be with you,
I've known inside me myself
                and you.
I've broken away
        from the suffering sea –
I'm flying to the start
            of all beginnings.

SOON – WAR

The War will soon be here! –
I can hardly breathe
         onto the Dust's pillow.
The seeds of the Lie –
Continue their atomic explosions .
The country of poverty,
Choking with the memory's unholy blight
              once again,
Prays to learn
When the abscess will be
         cut to pieces.

The War will soon be here! –
Perversions do blind by Naivety.
It's not possible to swaddle
The revivals with the follies of blisses.
It's not possible to disperse
The infinite ball of meanings
         with the blitzkrieg.
The War will soon be here! –
She's the collapse
        of honour and suffering...
There's a foray of new nobodies...

DRAWING

The Past jeers at the future,
Crosses are melted by smoke,
Meanings confess in the horrors' ward,
Debt stiffs at the uttermost line.
Reiterating my prayer in dream,
I stroll along brightness' outskirts again,
Drink trouble to draft the drawing
Of desperation on the heart-rending wall.

Generations are cut off by scalpel
Of volte-faces rotted through with guilt,
Haze's drawing above a pseudo country
Is erased by calque of time.

Repainting despair into hatred,
I knead the moment on evil's palette,
Cut to pieces crossroads of words
By treasons of those who knew
         without grasping shoots.
Having changed
           to imprint non-personal
On the infinite's arrow to null,
I set fire from
        the drawing to stars' condor
And return to my bothering role...

JANUARY

I am existing with the effort
                of will power
I am not waiting for kindness
                 and not giving it
I am not pining over the former days,
But I'm not liking the present ones.
I have endured all commotions,
I have become every guise.
I cannot whitewash myself
          from the dirt's remainders:
Having desired them so much.

I have been so tired to deal out
             the needless precepts,
To hope for the miracle,
To trust that I will not
Destroy everything again.
But it is not simple to leave myself,
How many times I have tried in vain.
I have hardly lived out
            the Autumn of Life –
So it is not far from its January.

REFUGE OF HOPES

There is the efflorescence of Naivety
On the hateful and delicate chains
Of tired feelings, formal caressings –
There are our children in it
Who are also not interested in us.
These are not us
      who have betrayed the ideas –
Let the fury drown in the mire of lie.
But our great-grandsons
             will dare to be alive
Till the dishonour only.
There is non-absoluteness of non-laws,
There is the hands' wood
            of the lying bonds
Which are begging
      for the tampons of the past
To convert the dye into blood,
The cemetery into a meadow.
Pity, there are no
           needless stops –
Maladies are curing,
Smoothing out they are beating us.
Becoming pale we are waiting
For changes, as though new ones –
This is the refuge of hopes.

DAWN OF MINE

Please do steal me
        from madness to night.
Oh! My Lord! Be ravaged, lead me away
Along infinite's shoots into twilight,
Into rotted through mucus of Time.

Can't survive evil's vow
        with lying remorse,
Can not waste that was unknown
How to conserve
        from Naiveness, imploring
Utterless not to whisper me end.

Dawn of mine drags along
        passing line again,
Predestined by Fate in vain
On the pilfered dreams and idylls:
Dawn of mine – is the near lonely star.

QUANTIZATION

Our time
Is quantized
By our songs,
Our perishable
Is revolted
By our welcomes –
Vomiting with primordially, dreams
Are overflowed
     with the soul's fanatical cruelties.
The delights
Are slipping away
After shadows,
Which are sticking
The quanta of time
Into Nothing.
The yelling Pain is germinating
          between offences –
We only need each other till death
The indifference –
To the justified
Infidelities,
Superperson –
On the wall
Of the supermind.
The interminableness
     of the vanishing blisses –
We are getting
          the Debts for the debts.

The perversion –
To the worn out
Lying feelings,
The revival –
To the naiveties
Which are scattered
On the mad waste
      of the heart-rendering Words –
They are alive with me,
No matter how much
         you will burn me.

CASTLE

The noble riff-raff
Is building the castle on the empty.
The withered humanity
Is soaring over the dome with a cross.

Wasting the caution on the smoulder
Of the imitated
Of oblivion's ice,
Risking to become
An everyday pronoun.

PHEOPHANIA'S NIGHT

Outside the window two birds
Were yelling into my meaning –
The cut ached,
The gibberish cried.
I was racing my moan –
The balcony infinite with ecstasy.

I'll have no time to have a drink,
I'll make myself sew the ardour together
From the Dream
To cool down,
To extort the cordiality for them:
The mirror-like surface
Of the apathetic heart-rending.

Outside the window two birds
Were tearing to pieces my life.
The Naivety was asleep
And alive with the Word.
Pheophania's night
Melts with the pain of the mind.

The fancy realm – begone!
The palette is slipping away –
I'm trying to burn the sheet
Which is the humus of my soul.
Stand up, do not waste your gaze
On the emptiness – there are debts
Which are waiting for their sacrifice.

WITHIN A HAIRSBREADTH OF LIFE

Yes, I have known
That I will not leave without purpose –
The moment's dream is full of delicacy, evil.
The arms of Fate, her eyes – almost alive –
Do not allow me to sing the words of madness.

I'm opening the nebula of gas as for the last,
Non-burning and desirable time:
I'm within a hairsbreadth of life –
The call in my doorway
Is putting off my execution for an hour.

There is the same deserted, rubber evening:
What does this hour give,
How many years has it stolen?
In case you have no things
By which to love and cry
Let your inside sonnet exhaust itself
With repetition.

STARS

Stars have been named,
         myths have been crushed:
I'm washing myself yelling lying truth.
I'm slipping away,
         I'm wounded by the dawn –
Tears have been dried out,
         children have been stolen.

Meanings have been cut off,
         gods have been poisoned:
I'm penetrating
         the Nothingness by Word.
I'm betrayed by the past,
         on the future lies the ice mask
Of the deal with Eternity –
         no time to waste.

HEATING

To my Mother...
I shall cover with tenderness
Your crisp grave.
There is the vast field
Of the crosses cut off –
I love it.

I shall tear off the virgin weeds
With the moan: «Forgive me».
I shall heat your sleep
With myself and the whispering:
«Please. Stop. Yes. Wait...»

FIGHTING

I'm fighting with the Past in Hysterics –
I'm rejecting the sweetmeat of Lies.
I'll cast away the sweep-net
                  of Happiness
Into Dreams' Sea for Passion and Sorrow
To be born from the grinning Naivety
Of the thrown about angry years –
In them I'll forget the melancholy
Of blisses which haven't been fulfilled.

I'll convert the Laughter into Distress –
This is a tiring theme.
Let the non-primordial desires' infinity
Be melted into the Nothingness.
I'm slipping away from the razor's blade
Of foam of poor words,
For the forthcoming debts' cloister
To be uncircumspectly destroyed.

TORTURE-CHAMBERS

The torture-chambers of the meanness
Are intimidating, aching,
Calling to the Nite.
Do pour your moans over sincerity
To melt in silence among them –
Let them be lying.

Do soften the humus's yelling
With wretchedness –
I'm crying
And kissing the ground.
I'll curtain the essence
With rays of constellations' light
To hover as outcast.

AFTER YOUTH

After youth I was delirious
                with childhood,
I didn't know where to run
                and how to live.
The reality threatened with scantiness,
Trying to poison me with poverty.
Rejecting hundreds of sure miseries,
Intuiting only the honest game,
Throwing the maxi-lives about,
I've comprehended
                the octopus of success.
But where is the infinities' dale
Which I was deriving
          from the formulas of dreams?
So only the depository
                of the inside sinfulness
Was caressing and coddling
                with the bottom's stench.
Oh! Truths rotted through with evil!
Do not reflect the unfinished world.
Shooting off with the leaves of youth
From the loneliness's rapier,
I'm oiling canvas with despondency,
Which is yelling, grounded by myself:
The gin of madness soldered
                in my soul
Is hysterically whispering:
            «Be with your Dream».

WITHOUT YOU

Without you – no reasons to live,
Without you – stars are washed off
With yelling of salty tears.
Without you – I don't try to open
Womanly bin,
Sprinkled to smell.

Without you – my Moment cools,
Without you – goals are lost
In poverty of inexperienced caresses.
Without you – I don't look
for Fate's thread
Which is cut off lengthwise,
Is eaten by the crowd-moth.

Without you – our World
can't be drunken,
Without you – ice-drifting
of angry nights
Melts the door into truth.

Without you – «to be» remains,
Not to soothe pain,
To recover, to rise.
Without you – no reasons to live...

LINE

You are – my line,
Symbols' handful,
You are – wall to «non-I»,
Forgive me again.

Dream's file by bytes
Expels gibberish
Interrupted by moan
Of those absent.

Yelling, reading tear
Of their despair,
Waiting thunderstorm
Of intersuffering,

I place my cross
On the screen to Nothingness,
Stopping Bottom's wrangle,
I transpose text.

You are – my line,
Symbols' handful,
You're – wall to «non-I»,
Forgive me again....

LEAVES

Peeping in my room
Leaves are shunted by sorrow,
Crossing out my living
By heart-rending whispering.

Tossing in hysterics, like a beast,
Letting all confidence – to walls,
I cry «beware!»
To immoderate longings.

They torment my insides,
My soul, and call to you –
So many reasons forcing me
To see or phone.

Covering myself with impossibility
To get closer to our past,
I stay to be alive
Behind my face distorted by grief.

CALL TO THE PAST

Do not call to the Past:
It is the frozen statues of feelings.
Do not call to the Past:
The eyelids where memories are
Only trembling to the crunch.

Let no good
Wait at a distance away from the dream:
The well-groomed
Facade of the lie
Will take away the gaze
From the bottom for a moment.

The worn-out wig of the years
Is pricking the eyes
With the needles of the days:
Do not call to the Past –
If you want to know
            the Cross of the Future.

FLIGHT

I love you, love you
Up to the deep heart spasm.
You are my poison desired,
You are my soul orgasm.

The lock of the uneasy years-days
During which we were apart,
They cry from the inside –
I have grown into yourself by pain.

The blinded blisses
Of the two supernovas –
It is a flight to the depth
Of two hearts, like roses.

SOUL

My soul,
Transparent from the pain,
Has suddenly abated
Near the precipice of years
It is sleeping
Lightly.
The mad feast
Of the debts
Is stinging to the screaming.
Is laying bare,
Rotting my depths.
Oh! No! Nay!
I didn't beat!
And I did not betray!

The lying meaning
Spilling on the motives,
Is laughing
At the wretched:
«Tender is the Night».
I was whitewashing
Anew the tears,
Freezing from power
Of prevision,
And have consumed it
With the Bottom's ray.
Oh! Yes! Yeah!
Refusing, I was waiting...

CLEANING

Accords of centuries
Are appealing in pangs
   To the scaffold to themselves.
Giving up the hatred
I'm bursting into the white sheet –
   Everywhere there is my Lord and me.
There are traits of His doctrine
In the doubt-dreams –
   Whether I perceive
      the knife of Nothing?
There is the guiltiness
From the wrong waste –
   That life – for a penny: Christ.
My prayer is spreading
To the home coast
   In defiance of passions.
By love of the Lord,
By caressing birch-rods
   I will cleanse my gaze
      to do it by myself.

MOON

Eyes of the Moon – are hazel:
I was so waiting for You
           evening and night,
Searching the mirage of the Past,
Endeavouring to surmount
           the whole of it.

Tears were smelling of alien,
For a moment, filtering to moan,
Deforming the principle how to glue
Delight from the crying sides.

Having shivered of strange avenues,
Having wasted the charge to live,
Expelling motif-glumness,
I forgave to wreathe Nothingness.

I made from by-gone tenderness
Your Image,
     having washed off entreaty
Remains of ailing years,
No powers to comprehend them.

Made currentless by You anew,
I've chosen not to trade with the Bottom
Profession-pain, the Loneliness,
To consume the volume in time.

REFLECTIONS

I expel my hatred
Into the basket for Passion –
Their strange devotion
Vexes night with pseudo happiness.
Escaping to sacrifice
Of revenge neglected,
Melting goals' bones
With honour wasted,

Grasping lie of flattery,
Affectedness of meanings,
Having died with fast dream,
Taking the knife of poverty,
Yelling, passing through
To stolen years pealed by thought,
Reiterating living's moment
By my childhood crushed,

Annoying earnest
With attempts to wash off gibberish,
Hinting into sincerity
To forget life's tender blisses,
Interrupting rally-parade
Of nonsensical myths,
I'm closing shatters to town
Of achievements without reefs.

BODY

Oh, Body! – You are an insecure shield
From the unsparing splashes of Life. My soul
Is sickened by Naiveness:
                    the AIDS of depths
Will absorb the aspirations
                        not to the end
And will erect the gravestone
                    of Reproach.

Oh, Meanings which are extorting Lies!
Do not protect
                the nakedness of the pattern
Of your facelessness.
When you understand
That you have taken
                    through robbery,
Laughing, the Fate is threatening
With starvation once again.

Be cold and separate the flight
Of the extorted
                    and utilitarian passion,
Do not be lost, while comprehending
The ford of fancy realm,
Adorn the dome of heaven
With the super sacrifice
To melt in them
With the unmeltable Happiness.

RENDEZVOUS

Anew I make a date for the Past
Having been gnawed by crowd
                  countless times,
By the dream of excuses,
Unwearying, warming myself
Over Fate painted by death.

I try to surmount the meaning
On which my soul's space is held,
I writhe in life's dance –
Bottom's flares
Scatter the night of Hatred.

I drink the estrangement's beverage,
Transparent and pestered,
Diluted with ring of tears.
My yelling is absorbed with intimacy –
I conceal the hollow-cheek
With the sheet warped by the line.

BLINDS ON THE YOUTH

The Night
Is losing her head
By letting out
Shadowy delights –
I follow suit.
It is impossible to overcome
Obstinacy of events
By the unconsciousness.

To edit
The abated
Cathedral of words
Hardly tinkling –
There is already
No time and evil.
The non-perishable
Soul's ashes
Are drawing
Blinds
On the youth.

PRAYER

Father-God!
Hide me from the sorrows around me
Father-God!
Don't allow me to have those dreams.
What should I do?
To start my life from the beginning?
How do You
Permit the crying from my depth?

Father-God!
Tell me where do you keep Dreams?
Have the goals,
Here, been really false?
Father-God!
Answer with no offense, who are You?
Maybe all the time
I'm crying and crying to myself?...

FULLMOON

I was making Heaven's way
        to the Fullmoon's moan,
I was growing faint
        from the bottom ineffableness
Of soul soften
        by the crucifixion of madness
Of our yelling mutual understanding.
To learn the length of the ray
        turned away by gibberish
Of Dreams which are not perverted
        by care –
And that is all, and my tears
        will stop to lie for Hope.
I shall shovel meanings
        to become cool.
I was making Heaven's way
        to the Fullmoon's moan:

The Star was calling,
My love has been burnt.
The power of the Grave –
Was taking things
Which belong to her.

When? I didn't know,
I was sleeping with my sadness,
And was making Heaven's way
To the Fullmoon's moan....

BROADWAY

Where are you, the winds
                of mad joys?
Where is the ardour
        of delights, sorrows, passions?
They have parked the divine trembling
Into the nonsense of fates –
This is the soul's Broadway.

Whose star's collapse is dragging
Into the black hole of the mob?
Whose poverty's crying is enveloped
With the shivers of fancy realm?
Who will fall into the Nothing
When the Depth's supply of words
Stops to turn up thoughts?

What will weaken the pity
            of the past and greed?
What will replace the sincere
                gibberish of Essence?
To turn out the tirelessness,
To make drunk the strangeness
With the primordial meaning
Which is absent?

PULLING

Pulling a face
I'm drinking again
The space without you,
And waiting,
When
Your,
Watering with Dream,
Gaze,
Wearing the belly of malice,
Gives birth
To the composition,
Discarding nulls.

Please, cover us
With the Passion throw,
And do not set congeal
In the artificial night,
Moving backwards to the glow
Of the lying leprousness.
Please, take me
For your second brush
To become my third
Dream superhemisphere.

COAST

The coast of my gibberish is cut up
By neglectfulness of senses.
I'll burn my sinfulness to pay
      my debts in the night.

I'll soften in the color of lines
Of the thrown-away idylls –
I'll forget the Passion cry.

I'll carry out His words
And take her white-lie kisses –
I'll beautify my crypt with anguish.

I'm not afraid of destroying Hope,
I'll let out my moan to them
Before I find the final peace.

Skinned by Him, all infinities
Are ground
      on the table
         of my soul's dream –
The realms
      of fancy
         are lapped by vileness:
Weeping is an echo
      from the unknown Abyss...

ILLUSION

Refugees of pity –
The Thread over the abyss is cut.
The Past is split lengthwise:
Extends alongside.
Tumour is turning
To moan, within a wall
Of Sore Time.
Sweetness of fancies fattened,
Pride in the empty,
Lassitude of engine-desires
Up to ashes.
Illusion-consolation,
Joy of unbound molecules
Which the wind of chance
Composes into initials down the Bottom
Like specks of dust
Smelling with cinders of arguments
And dirty tricks.

BONE

I'm throwing away
A bone to Fate
For being permitted
To be in the impetuous city.
Repressing the peace and pride,
I'm trying to set ajar
The cage into the World
Of dreams distorted.
Do stop the super-moan
Of madness.
Everything –
To be forgotten!
Break up the pain
Of the mind's exhaustion
Into the drops.
Waste up the empty role
Which has named herself as life.
Do weave
The throw of the fancy realm –
The wisdom –
From the word's infinity
For not pushing aside
A Moment into the oblivion's ditch.
Do shorten out
The power of the Lie
On the melancholy's weakness.
Please, take me: change
Death – into gladness.

GETTING COLD

I want to get cold
                by loneliness so much,
But you are bringing me
                temptations in your hearts.
I am preparing myself to be consumed
                by super creativity –
My eyes are blinded up
                with pins' flirtation in your hair.

I'm sounding the alarm
                about the Time's loss –
They're offering me
                the poverty's AIDS.
How not to regain consciousness
                under the Naivety's tree,
How not to waste my Mind
                for the Dream and Mode of Life?

Do not bring out the odor
                of the all-permission,
Don't kill the shadow
                you don't know whose it is.
Travelling all over the infinity Bottom
                of Conscience,
I'm simply loving each
                of you as before.

DUET

Our mutual running
One into the other is disconsolate,
It is full of rebukes,
        is craving and tender:
Being jealous we're waiting.

The view of the coast is colored
With insatiableness –
We'll sing a duet to life's cough.
The revelling of dreams is careful –
If not that, who will help
To attain yourself.

The wounds of guiltiness are enticing
Into the brilliant traps
To embrace in a crunch.
I'm praying: for us, it's impossible
Not to become living steel.

Goddess of tears!
  Do weave from roses
    The carpet of primordiality,
        The fate and blessing!

THREE CEMETERIES

The end is burning –
The conception is melting
You cannot condescend
To yourself from the Bottom.
Farewell the over-fervid world,
Scoffing with the
                    pseudo vitality's dream
Near the window
          of the untouched illusion –
The cemetery-rooms
Are attracted by the Love,
The Childhood and the Natal.
Their anxiety,
The fancy realm of the loneliness,
The Nothing's kissing,
As the smoke of the non-parting,
Allow me to cross fire –
It is not successful
To be rid of my footprint.
I'm rousing my conscience
With the leafing over of the inside
So not to hear the trivial reply:

Life is the multidimensional cemetery
With the right of going there only
From the clammy infinity of the passage
Into my yelling lonely confinement
Which is finely connected with the world
By the threads of the soul's
Refined verse-formulae.

I HAVEN'T NOTICED

I haven't noticed the senility –
Nobody calls me and nobody asks me.
My own children are taking
Their children to the kindergarten.

I've tired of running, but the memory
Can be wiped by Nothingness only.
There are no events –
                            there are no reasons
For my soul to ail with the years.

I have poured myself over the Past,
But the pain has not been abated:
There is the rubber of my nights...
There is the cold of my bed...

DOWNPOUR

Downpour – by the window,
Snow – inside me.
Selection of mine:
Let you – Sin.

Fire – to my back,
Sheaf – of betrayals.
Edge – near me,
Stop – of Naivety.

On my table, a list
Of mundane affairs,
Splash of ideas,
Sonnets that have been sung.

Downpour – by the window,
Snow – inside me...

IN THE CITY

In the wild city
Disemboweled with poverty
It is better to be proud
Then to be over-fed.

Where should I go? –
To the betrayer-Nite.
The Shadows are squeezing my soul
And governing my goals.

If I knew my own limits –
I'd be laughing boisterously,
I'd want to spit
On my false fate.

Do learn more rapidly –
Is it worth living or nonliving?
The row of my insolent roles
Germinates into Disgrace...

SURMISE

The light was glimmering
I shall not leave in vain.
No!
My Meaning has been sung
By the layers of the years
Squeezed the poverty.
I'll heat the Moan
Guilty with the secular
Wasted –
A super-chime
Has deafened
The fancy realm
With peals,
I am overwhelmed
By the surmise:
Is it He or is it not He?..

EMBRACING

Everlasting the inevitableness,
Learning, submissively,
About the day,
When the successfulness,
As the pseudosinful,
To me appears as a virgin,
I'll slip into the past to tears,
Fighting my soul, coloring my pain,
To not burn up, from life the gathering
Of the unpremeditated replete,
Of the uncalmless wicked –
I'll burn down with prayer,
As the blade of the gibberish,
That World which I have not embraced
Alone.

EVENING'S FADE

The evening's fade
Has come in and is waiting.
I'm crying, driving it away,
Frustrated – it is useless.

It will promote
The black conceptions' domain,
It will shovel – the past,
It will burn up brightness,
Smooth out the nimbus
And damage my dreams.

Stand still!
The cyclic-moan unlimited.
I'm going out,
Going for the candles....

FEVER

Being held in the ice-hole
          of the inconsolable,
I shall come to myself.
I shall try to lie on the brazier
          not to burn
The mental city of mine
          with its uselessness.

I'll tear off hatred from heartlessness,
I'll get even with everyone
          who has lied,
I'll braid fancy realm and gibberish
          into the cloth of feelings
So no one kisses me ever.

I'll back off from the window only
          to take a running start,
I'll embrace to forget you fast,
I shan't know for whom I was crying
          for years.
Are you passing away? –
          It is simply a fever.

RADIATION

My air –
Is the blinding flow of radiation.
I gnaw it –
And my life is wiped out by X-rays.
No!
I don't want to decay on atoms!
Do I go that way? –
We are blamelessly squeezed.

The quiet and calm:
"What's the matter, don't be afraid..."
By what do you measure everything?
You cannot get round
The childish prattle
And trembling of essence
By the faith in the degrees of lie.
So who is to be responsible?...

POINT

Being tortured with lie,
I was alive with you –
The lies' superlayer
Between us
Consumed the cut
To the impossible.
The couch has been built –
Then I break into rage towards myself
And go to my crypt-dungeon.
Because I see that my moan
Isn't needed here –
I'll disperse my haughtiness
On the faces of words.

The crowd made me sick –
I'm standing up straight
In front of the worst
I'll reject the flattery
Which is the tsarina of dreams.
I am tired
To exhaustion
By the poverty of the sounds.
Where do I find
The promises of years?
The passionate and silly,
Alien lips of love
Cannot be torn away
From the dead blisses.

The footprint
Of the Naivety –
Rib crunch – is over –
The gibberish
Has mounted the moment.
There is a row
Of Dream-like gravestones –
The light gapes
Out of the verse's point...

GOAL

I am madly happy –
       there is loneliness.
What I was striving for –
       I've already attained.
I do not want to embrace
       the Lie of calmless.
The Meaning of life
    has appeared as the bottom's ash.

It is not
       in work and wives,
In children
       and appointments:
It's only
    in the changing
            movement of the Mind –
But let the mortals –
       forgive me.

PLAYHALL

I have examined everybody –
And what is the result? –
The playhall was converting
The heart-rending
Into the good-for-nothing of the humus.
Turning away
The grin of Eternity,
Became white with frost,
The illusions' ball
Was betraying life
With delight,
Having travelled
Over all facets,
Putting together
Forces and dreams
Into the Naivety
Inviolable with ashes,
I have prayed again suffering,
I have bitten through the longings
For my imperceptible crying
To congeal into the Future.

FLOWERS

Touching the flowers
Of neglectfulness
They sang
The meaning of revival
For lost purposes,
Motifs of the sincere
And weary Dream
Burnt down by the vital juice
As the echoes of the void
To wane in moan.

In one thrown in the immenseness
Of the icy lonely cage.
On hands and knees from tenderness
Poisoned centuries.
Give the inside scope to souls
To the illnesses of the conscience.
The verse covered with sadness
Is the tombstone-reproach
For them –
Which has been irradiated
By dreams.

BALL

The varicolored ball of smell of dreams
Has been torn away.
My soul
Is not begging for the things
Which have gone away.
Crying,
The senility is gnawing at me –
Frost is on my skin.

The Nite of pseudo-Life
Is mowing her crop
And carrying off my Meaning
To the exhausting Couch,
To multiply my shout with yelling,
To multiply my mark with trace....

Oh! My Lord...
        My Lord...
                My Lord...

HATRED

I'll cut off hatred from sorrow,
I'll be swaddled into the chime
Of the wasted years – who needs
The poverty's moan,
Having eaten away the memory?

I'm thrusting into myself
The fatigued gaze,
I'm accusing my depths –
Which forces will caress
And give me to breathe once again.

A moment has been added
Into the grave of moments –
They fill ill, they are living
In those who believe,
That the first moment and the last one
Were given for them only.

BEND

There's the bend
Of the Fate's thread –
The blow is sliding
On the Mode of life.
Oh! My Lord!
Do not catch me
On the sincere word
Of love,
Do not stand
Around ahead
Of the non-living.
Please, open your eyes
To the Poverty –
I'm tired to burn down
To the Bottom
My last ray inside me.
I'll force
The stains to be washed
By the offenses'
Calmness
Of the obscene
Reproach.
I'm crying, praying,
I'm waiting
For the terror-day:
The Nite is scoffing at me –
I'll get drunk with the oblivion.

GAZE

The gaze abandon
By the promises – she's lying.
The garden
Of Fate dead – I shall sing it
To its ashes.
Was it a running start? –
The running in the circle...
The bars of passing years
Are closing out the light
To be changed into a resilient bed.
The flight's – the fever,
I'll be washed by evil.
Let the flagstaff
Of Past delights –
Be through and gone.
To be with the needless rhyme
Of Life,
As with the solitary cell
Of dream, apart.
The only Image
Inviolable –
Is pseudo narcosis.
Here is a switch –
The turning of it...
Has sweared the moment
Over the empty Universe.

HORIZON

My horizon is torn to pieces –
The crucifix was made by lead.
I do not hear the Singing.
The Fall love – full of ice
Is warping and warping my dream.
Let me discard
That which no longer suits me.
I am divorced with the false
Inside of me.
The thing, which is
A captivity,
Is my morgue of happiness,
As the Naivety's vineyard
Deceased in the rime of Dream.
The smoke of time
Has only enveloped – the Call,
Reminding with its odour
That my ardour,
Being accumulated up
By Neglectfulness,
Is my soul's mad horseman
Exhausted by the worst evil
Of all-devouring
And needless words.

BURNING UP THE LIFE

Burning up the life
Is trampling my Light
In her embrace,
Throwing into the furnace
Of already other's years
The pain-shed bits amputated
From the mutilated soul.
Oh! No!
The sweet Naivety and the blindness
Will not give them back to the call:
There is the Time's dart-killer –
Who, piercing, gives you more.
It was long ago desired
To yell: «Yes!»
Towards the fetid
Ditch of Dreams.
Do burn up now –
It does not matter –
I'll over-bear
The remains of the vanishing life,
I am exhausted...
I'm hoary with ages...
I'm melted....

CLOT

Blind with my dream-ruins
Of broken years and goals,
Get stronger with the word «senility»,
I'm kneading the clot
Of the soul's unleavened wares
Nursed with foam from the mob
To satiate life's last volume
With stench.
I will drink the heart-rending
Corpse's debts, achievements
Squeezed in luxurious paws
Of Fate lying to your face,
I cut off the terror's remainder,
I burn up the Root by my doubt
To powder with ashes
The path to nowhere – to be....

HAVING

Having extorted the meaning,
Stand still for exaltation –
There is an awful lot of crushing
Of the handful of living.

The grin of the unwinking,
The reproach of the saints –
I'm bearing the moment
Into the morbid ground.

The guiltiness
Will absorb the yelling about
Everything having been wasted –
At the end:
Me – an old man.

Face will be opened
For the last time –
The Things which were stored up
Will be whitewashed with Prayer.

PLAYING THE GAME

The callous voice
Of the inviolable Dream
Is heard in the Night –
Her rotten pieces
Are caressing my throat.
The graphomaniacs' chorus
Is spattered with evil.
My yelling is –
Not the damp of bottom rhymes
And not the house of verses
Of trite and miserable metres:
Being tipsy with my pain
I drink myself,
Extorting from my soul
The meaning
Of what I have been here,
Why I have wasted all my roles,
Why I was swimming
In the wrong direction
And rowing with the false oar? –
Yeah, I was simply living...
Was praying...
And was freezing
Playing the game of change.

LIFE

I am not full from the delight
                    of my prayer
And I have shrunken.
What have I done? – The old man
Is dispersed by hopelessness.
The restlessness –
The mind's evil – reigns not there.
The inhuman delicacy
Is not the Ray. Please, answer!

Who is there? – The immenseness
Of the morbid bondage.
Oh! Priestess of dreams! –
You are being poured over me
From head to foot by the nightmare.
You are a lover
Of the inconsolable and meek
Corpses –
Life!

FEAST OF LONELINESS

The ardour was wintering –
Inside me my soul was driving.
Whither? – I didn't know.
She was counting out –
I was counting on:
And it did not tally...
And the Malice,
Softening with Passion psalms,
Squeezing her grin, rushed.
It was a stinking and eternal Ball,
Orgies of caresses,
The feast of loneliness –
And the Salvation.

BEING DELIRIOUS

Being delirious by despair
I shall burn up with nonsense
The whole World! –
The settling tank
Of poverty's perfection,
The inexhaustible
Is spattered with ashes,
The sick old man
Is embracing the madness –
He knows, knows, knows...
Making the palette
From the entire blackness
And pain,
The rejecting comes in a hurry.
Oh! Make your brush
More fine – you see I am alive.

CHARRED NIMBUS

The charred nimbus
Has cut up
The absolute meaning –
Throughout.
The peace exhausted
Was shredding
The whole inside of me
To pieces –
Layer after layer:
Let evil come
Into the poverty.
The waste land
Was calling to the Nothing –
Step after step.
The power of the lie
Is delight.
The finality
 Was taking years of moan way
Let the sweetmeat of Naivety
Come to the reproach.

SCYTHE OF TIME

Oh! You! The scythe of Time!
Do stand still!
Oh! You! The blade of Nothing,
Set to the fancy realm –
Be frozen to dream
About yourself in future,
To know that my footprint
Has not melted,
That I
Have not been successful
In lying.
Oh! You! The Goddess of wisdom,
Senility!
Remove me
From the spears of the naive words –
As prickles in the roses
Desired –
Consume my Mind
For the delight
Of unpredicted steps
Behind the horizon,
Their empty peal
Will come.
But what's for me?
Why me?
I'm finished....

HIGH WORDS WITH MY MOTHER NEAR HER GRAVE

I am coming to you in the snow a metre deep. The wind with snow – into my face too. As if it is angry. My every step is a half of myself. I am falling, rising, going straight on and on again. I knew that these high words were to be said. And they have been uttered.

With every step of mine I was going through your whole life. And I have gone through it.

I have understood everything. Your loneliness, sufferings, aspirations and blows, our blows. Living with us, you were alone thrice. You were knocking without result into our souls, closed. And I was afraid of your eyes, longing to us, to our understanding and sympathy. In them there was our salvation.

Now I am reliving your life. I am doing the same things with the same end. This is your revenge, delayed. What for? So that I were rushing about among women all my life, discovering a part of you in them, trying to redeem my fault before you, worrying and suffering with them as you have been doing the same with us, in search of things which were not received from you for my impregnable misunderstanding. Yes, I have been doing this for so many years. Till today. I have been melting your revenge which is already not malicious and offended. In my love to you. In my understanding of you. Of the fact that namely me – is the man with whom you could have found the things you have been seeking for a long time, with whom you could have been really intimate. I have accepted you and understood you. But I have been late for just seven years. Only now, on the day of the seven-years since your death. Is it too late? No. Once again no. You know, this may not have happened at all.

I have removed the snow from your grave, giving you a possibility to breathe a little and to talk with me. I have been cleared up your picture and kissed you into your lips. I would so much like to embrace you alive. For the first time in my life. Very much. Truly.

Do you see that I am crying? Never mind. You see, these are the my first tears for you. Going away, I told you: "I shall change myself, you will see, I shall change". And then: "I shall come to you, wait for me". For the first time in my life I didn't feel like leaving you. There, behind the windy snow field, the strange city and alien living were waiting for me, but there the main thing was lacking – there was no YOU.

TIME

He is Time. Trying to deceive yourself. To fill yourself if only with anything. Not with a look into yourself. Over there it is not O.K. The intercourse is in vain, with void. By void. I am quiet alone. I am all by myself. But in the compulsory presence. There is vacuum. Around me. Inside me. I am struggling in my search of Him. But what for? And what of Him? Well, there is the abundance of Him. The whole day. And what is then? What is inside? Where is the motion of myself? Where is me? Where is my ego? Nothing but the torments of the Nothingness.

The life is boiling outside the window. It is the pseudolife.

They are also trying to annihilate Him. Without feelings. There have dozens of imaginary businesses. To read everything. What for? To feel everything? What for? Not to know His inexorable rhythm.

There is the Hope, not for the present. She is like the straw dragging you to the Bottom. And there is no way backwards. Till you hope.

CRUSHEDNESS

The Night – is the slave of the Death. Day after day dying in the hope to turn out different the next morning. Seemingly different. Dream – is the swallower of our aspirations. I hate it. But where am I to go?

The Sheet – is the scope of the unvoicedness. Who needs it? Before whom? And what for? There is this clot of excuses. For the undone.

The vice and virtue – where are they? In deeds? In ideas? In conceptions? – In the understanding of the essence. In the touch of the integrity, in the flow of life. Does a man smoke, who has swallowed up smoke under the whooping of the crowd "And you are sinful" too? Perhaps he laughs at the joy of the primitive understanding, that is, over the misunderstanding of all. The vice is a power over the human. It does not matter, what this power is. But any power – is already a vice. The circle has been closed.

YOUR DYING INSIDE ME

Well, I have gone through Your dying till Your death. Nothing to write about further. Point. But, no! The infinity is inside this point. Which cannot be avoided. The wedding air. Let it be damned. Is it for keeps or no? It is just necessary to breathe. What for? My accursed imagination. What should I do with it? To imagine everything without You? There is senselessness and emptiness in the rest. Which for?

Well, I have gone through Your motionless decease. The sufferings. Ours. Dreams. The expression of my face has been changed. Squeezed by the grimace of doom, that is not melted in the crowd and excites sympathetic looks which I do not see, but feel. Using my energy I push everybody apart and tear along to You. Only You. Now, it is quite clear for whom that charge of care having been saved up, which is thrown about to children by other unforgotten moral admonitions, ostentatious caresses and the excrements of their complexes. But for the beloved there are lies and the one-minute readiness for betrayal and faithlessness. If only nobody knows. And everything is allowed. And anxiety? Is it sincere even if sometimes? I imagine everything. And You are at my place. And You are moving one hand only. And you are creating. I am waiting. You are speaking. You call the number of the brush. We are mixing in the needed color. And we are creating. The things which are told by Him. The Reality? Nothing of Her. She is only a child born from the Dream and the desire to disappear. O.K. Let Her live. There is little to remain. How to deaden this pain-sovereign of the soul? My vodka – is a computer screen. I am feeling through it. It is easier to breathe. And – as if some meaning were giving rise. My vodka – are semigroups.

But they do not save me either. I am catching at a guitar – the last straw. Nay. It is not what is needed. And just Your call. It is filled with the something different. For the first time You are not near me, but You – are here. Around. And inside everything.

I am drinking Your death to the dregs. There is no better beverage of roses. They, as if dead, stay in our vase, accumulating together with our celebrations. Waiting for the last drop. Do not hope...

PSEUDO

Every Friday you inevitably come to me again. Pseudo sex is on our schedule. The third lecture. With me. No missing classes. There are orgasms, orgasms and orgasms over and over again. But what are they to me? They are your self orgasms. They are empty, you know. In them the main thing is skipped – Love. Even the crumb of it, hardly breathing, slightly warm. Yeah. You caress yourself and caress me with your pseudo care. But whom? As you say, you caress me for yourself. What means you caress yourself and me? Where am I after all? I am housed into your next and now grown-up puppet, lifeless, with a penis. I will never agree. Not on my life. You are even afraid of talking about love. Because there is nothing to discuss. There is no topic for conversation. Neither there is feeling. You have admitted this yourself. But I have known it since our very beginning. And I am suffering. I am not be able to finish catching your fancy role of the cold-hearted doll. A supplier of empty orgasms – it is not for me. Thank goodness, that monkey age has already passed flying by the window of my youth, when physiology substituted for everything. But now only this is not enough for me. Moreover, it is so sickish undiluted that it can be disgusting. Did you notice it? Why can I not kiss your lips? Certainly, nay. For, according to you, the physiological satisfaction is the only thing the man can give you.

First – his penis like a piston. Till the yelling pain. Then – a tongue and a finger. Till the drawing of the mouth and convulsions. But what is next? Everything from the beginning. And – without feelings. And – without any hope for mutual penetration. Only – selfdouche with your own defecations – material and emotional. What a beggar you are! And – unhappy

123

one. Though you, naive, claim quite the opposite. Though you are delighted that you feel O.K. for two days after our meeting. But "I am satisfied" does not mean "I am happy" at all. And have you asked me, what is happening to me within these two days? Why do I feel so basely and vile? Why am I on the edge? The answer is simple. Because I love.

Not you. But Her. And you know whom. After all She – invisibly present, She – is always near us, She – is inside of me, in the soul of mine. And you feel it. And you are irritated.

But I am grateful to you. For I have realized it conclusively: this is mutually useful. You are using me as a mechanical irritant and a lifeless executor of your primitive desires. I am using you as a woman whom I knew earlier than Her. And here we are: I have lost my way in the wood of "close" and "distant". And I understood that the latter is less powerful than the former. Yes. Why did I call you up for six years after our parting? Perhaps I hoped that you could replace for Her? You are so much alike. But now I have made sure that this likeness is only superficial. I do not know. Perhaps I am guilty myself? For what are my poems, songs and Her paintings to you? It is a pity that you do understand nothing in them, neither a line nor a touch. All of them are transparent for you. Or it is not a pity? Behind them in your imagination you see the reflection of a penis, thickets of pseudo orgasms, and amusements, enjoyment, as a solid wall of the mutual estrangement. But I see a regular disillusionment and the abyss...

Every Friday you come again... Inevitably...

Poems in French

POEPHYSIQUE

La Poésie, un météore de sentiments. La Physique, un météore d'idées. Un nouveau chapelet de lettres, un nouveau chapelet de symboles mathématiques sont les deux faces de la Lune, un binôme étranger. Derrière mon âme, ils forment un Sphinx. Je ne sépare pas les idées de la Physique et les métaphores de la Poésie. La froide fusion incontrôlable est nécessaire à mon cœur pour les créer. Plus nouveau est le combustible, plus lois dais le Futur via le tir.

Je crois que la Poésie ne peut être construite comme une formule. Les règles externes sont transparentes pour Elle, et seules les règles internes sont vivantes. La seule règle vraie: sans une masse critique la réaction de la Créativité ne se fait pas. Les sentiments et les idées s'effondrent à de telles densités qu'indépendamment de mon désir, il y à une explosion dans l'Infini.

Ils sont interpénétrants. Je ne suis tour simplement pas capable de les éviter, et je n'ai plus peur que quiconque rie de ma faiblesse, de mes souffrances, de mes complexes, de mes défauts.

La Poephysique me permet de n'élever au delà d'eux, au delà de la ire, au delà du Tempo.

Traduction française: Christine Clairmont

OU ES-TU?

Où êtes-vous, Vents des joies infernales ?
Où est l'ardeur des délices, celle des peines et des
passions ?
Ils ont relégué la divinité tremblante
Dans le non-sens des destins –
Voici le Broadway des âmes
Quelle chute d'étoile t'entraîne donc
Dans le trou noir de la foule ?
Quel est ce cri de pauvreté qui t'enveloppe
Dans le frisson du royaume des illusions ?
Qui tombera dans le Néant
Lorsque les mots des Profondeurs
Cessent de dévoiler les pensées ?
A l'aide de quoi affaiblira-t-on la pitié du passé et
L'avidité
Avec quoi remplacera-t-on le charabia sincère de
L'Essence ?
Pour transformer l'inconstance
Pour soûler l'étrange
De vérités essentielles
Ce qui est absent ?

Traduction française: V. Morillon.

128

VOL

Je t'aime, je t'aime
Jusqu'au spasme demier du coeur.
Tu es mon poison chéri,
L'orgasme de mon âme.
Le verrou des années-jours difficiles
Durant lesquels nous avons été séparés,
Ils hurlent au fond de moi –
La douleur m'a fait grandir en Toi.
Les bonheurs aveugles
De deux supemovas –
C'est un vol en direction des profondeurs
De deux coeurs, semblables â des roses.

Traduction française: V. Morillon.

PLEINE LUNE

J'accomplissais un celeste chemin vers
                              les plaintes de la lune,
Je me sentais allege dans l'ineffable creux
De l'âme adoucie par la crucificion de démence
En notre comprehension mutuelle criante.
Pour apprendre la longeur du rayon tourné
                              par le balboutiement
Du rêve nullement perverti par l'inequiétude –
Et cèla est tout, et mes déchirements finissent
                              de mentir à l'espoir.
Je dois consentir l'acceptation pour découvrir
                              la paix.
J'accomplissais un celeste chemin vers
                              les plaintes de la lune:
A la supplique des étoiles
Mon amour fut brûlé.
Le pouvoir de la Tombe…
Prenait les choses
Qui lui appartenaient.
Quand? Je ne puis le savoir.
Je dormais imprégné de mélancolie
Et j'accomplissais un celeste chemin vers
          les plaintes de la pleine lune

Traduction française: Paul Cariage.

130

REVE

J'ai rêvé à la nuit –
Au jardin de tombes.
A deux pas – Plus loin
Lâ où vont les dettes de mon âme.
Le nimbus a fondu Je prie – Lis
Avec un gémissement. Ce hurlement d'un instant,
Reste tranquille N'aie pas l'audace de partir
Vie cyclotron En dissimulant ton visage.
Je prie pour que le Rêve inonde
La signification stagnante
Afin de réduire en poussière
L'encore du Destin.
Pardonne mon naufrage
Et mes échecs, la vente de mon âme
C'est le Délire –
A moi le Travail, le Foyer, la Morgue.
Je me suis éveillé de pierre –
Un rayon glisse
Du fond de la folie
J'en garderai l'impact en moi.
La Naiveté ronge, blesse, venge.
Mon pêché est détrôné
 – Royaume des illusions SIDA.

Traduction française: V. Morillon.

131

LUNE

Les yeux de la Lune – sont noisettes
Je t'espérais soir et nuit,
Tout en sondant les mirage du Passé,
Et en luttant pour en triompher.
Mes larmes avaient un goût étrange,
Un instant, cherchant à filtrer une plainte,
S'étirant comme un filet de colle
Délice des côtés en larmes.
Ayant frissonné sur d'étranges avenues,
Ayant gaspillé la force de vivre,
J'ai refoulé d'un air maussade des motifs,
Et oublié de lisser le Néant.
J'ai fait naître de la Tendresse passée
Ton image, après avoir effacé les supplications
Les restes des années douloureuses,
Aucune force ne peut les comprendre.
Tu m'as fait renaître un jour
J'ai choisi sans marchander avec l'Enfer
Une bien douloureuse profession, la Solitude,
Afin de consommer le volume du Temps.

Traduction française: V. Morillon.

132

APPEL AU PASSE

N'en appelle pas au Passé:
Statue figée des sentiments.
N'en appelle pas au Passé
Les paupières du souvenir
Se ferm,ent en tremblant au moment critique.
Ne laisse pas le bien
Attendre loin du rêve
Bien entretenue
La facade du mensonge
Entraînera un instant
Le regard loin du fond.
La perruque usagée des années
Pique les yeux
A l'aide des aiguilles des jours
N'en appelle pas au Passé –
Si tu veux découvrir le chemin du futur.

Traduction française: V. Morillon.

SEMI

Semi vérité et semi conscience,
Semi arguments et semi vie.
Semi monde ? – Cela ne vaut pas le Destin.
Semi mimoire ? – Disparue J'ai oublié.
Telle la libération des âmes.
"Semi" dissout le cercle de la significatin.
Sous le semi reproche d'un semi ennemi
Se cache le mensonge d'un semi ami.
Vendue avec des semi sentiments,
La nourriture est semi finie.
Semi mari – Semi frère
Semi rempli par un semi amour.
Un semi pouvoir est une senü liberté,
Tous ont honte et ne se plaignent pas.
Senü attentions réjouissantes
Nous sommes semi endormis.
Nouveau retour en arrière ?

Traduction française: V. Morillon.

INFINIE REDEMPTION

Dans ce monde,
Comme sur le rebord d'une larne,
Je suis une fois encore repris per l'air de l'Ame.
En souriant, je fus repoussé par les pertes.
Que reste-t-il de moi ? L'écriture.
Que devrais-je écrire alors que les Temps difficiles
Se font connaître sitôt disparus.
J'ai cru à ma chance mais tout le monde m'abandonne,
Mon reflet ressemble à un squelette blanchi.
Je fais mon lit pour deux
Pour eux, dans mon rêve,
Jusqu'au matin je préserve en vain ma chaleur.
Quoi, je ne serai ni l'un ni l'autre.
A ce moment, fou de terreur,
Je couvrirai mon papier d'Infini.
Peut-être s'agit-il de leur Rédemption
Je boirai tout ce qui refroidit
Jusqu'à la lie.
Dans ce monde,
Comme sur le rebord d'une lame ...

Traduction française: V. Morillon.

135

MON AUBE

Je t'en prie ne me soustrais pas à la folie de la nuit.
Oh ! Seigneur ! Etre dévasté, entraîné
Le long des rivages infinis jusqu'au crépuscule,
Etre décomposé par le mucus du Temps.
Je ne peux survivre au serment du mal avec de faux remords,
Je ne peux gaspiller l'inconnu
Comment se préserver de l'incredulité en implorant
Le Néant de ne finalenient rien me murmurer.
Mon aube m'entraîne de nouveau de l'autre côté de la frontière,
En vain voué au Destin
De rêves volés en idylles:
Mon aube – proche d'une étoile solitaire.

Traduction française: V. Morillon.

AVERSE

Averse – Par la fenêtre,
Neige – En moi.
Mon choix:
Pour toi – Pêché.
Feu – Derrière,
Faisceau – De trahisons.
Précipice – Près de moi,
Arrêt – Naiveté.
Sur ma table, une liste
D'affaires banales
Tourbillort d'idees
Un sonnet – Déjà chanté.
Averse – Par la fenêtre,
Neige – En moi ...

Traduction française: V. Morillon.

PASSAGER

Je ne suis qu'un curieux passager
Dans un train pour Nulle Part,
Des haltes dans des appartements glacés
Et des recherches infructueuses m'ont épuisées.
Oublié, amusé, anxieux
Mon haleine n'embue pas la fenêtre.
Les bas-côtés sans fin, ennuyeux et fatiguants –
Symbolisent l'inévitable.
Terre endormie – patient cimetière
Bardé de croix,
De leurs griffes acérées les pattes lumineuses des démons
Ecrasent mon âme qui ne laisse
                    plus échapper que des cris futiles.
Le vent de l'instant éparpille les espoirs,
Personne ne caresse dé ;jà plus ma douleur,
Dans mes yeux comme à l'abri de volets blancs,
Se terre l'angoisse infinie de la vie.

Traduction française: V. Morillon.

RADIATION

Mon air –
N'est que le flot aveugle de la radiation,
Je le ronge –
Et ma vie est balayée par les rayons X.
Non !
Je ne veux pas me désintégrer tel un atome
Est-ce que j'en prends le chemin ?
Nous sommes asphyxiés de facon irréprochable.
La paix et le calme:
"Que se passe-t-il ? N'aie pas peur..."
A l'aide de quoi mesures-tu toute chose ?
Tu ne peux échapper
Ni au babillage enfantin
Ni au tremblement de l'essence
En ayant foi en tous les degrés du mensonge.
Alors, qui doit être tenu pour responsable ?

Traduction française: V. Morillon.

* * *

Le coût de mon charabia est affecté
Par la négligence des sens
Je brûlerai mes idées pour payer mes dettes à la nuit,
Je brûlerai mes idées pour payer mes dettes à la nuit.
J'adoucirai la couleur des lignes
Des idylles perdues –
J'oublierai le cri de la passion,
J'oublierai le cri de la passion.
J'exécuterai ses ordres
Et accepterai ses baisers blancs de mensonge –
J'embellirai la crypte de mon angoisse,
J'embellirai la crypte de mon angoisse.
Je n'ai pas peur de l'espoir destructeur,
Je laisserai échapper un gémissement dans sa direction
Avant de trouver enfin la paix,
Avant de trouver enfin la paix.
Dépecés par Lui, tous les infinis
Sont à terre
Sur la table
Du rêve de mon âme –
Les royaumes
De l'illusion
Sont en proie à la vilénie
L'écho des larmes se répercute
　　　　　　　　　　au fond d'un Abîme inconnu.

Traduction française: V. Morillon.

140

DANS UN SOUFFLE DE VIE

Oui, j'ai appris
Que je ne vivrai pas sans but –
Le rêve de l'instant est empli de délicatesse, de mal.
Les armes du Destin, ses yeux – presque vivants –
Ne me permettent pas de chanter les mots
De la folie.
J'ouvre la nébuleuse du gaz pour les derniers,
Temps ininflammable et désirable:
Je me trouve à l'intérieur d'un souffle de vie –
Cet appel dans l'entrée
Retarde d'une heure l'exécution.
C'est toujoun le même soir déserté et caoutchouteux:
Qu'apporte cet heure,
Combien d'années a-t-elle volées ?
Dans le cas où tu n'aurais rien ni personne
A aimer ou pour qui pleurer
Laisse ton sonnet intérieur s'épuiser
A force de répétition.

Traduction française: V. Morillon.

141

* * *

Je me tiens en lanmes près de la fenêtre –
De toute part environné par un silence cruel
Le cri du coeur se mêle à la nuit,
M'arrachant ainsi mon espoir féminin.
Le temps se venge de mon rôle mensonger –
Mon coeur sait mais comment brûler mes échecs ?
Le téléphone s'est fait avoir par la mort –
Je suis veuf de ma bien-aimée.
Ne me jete pas mon passé au visage, j'embrasse le sol
Mais que puis-je donc faire ? Me refroidir à jamais ?
Le charabia s'insinue jusqu'aux tréfonds de mon âme.
Comment ne pas gaspiller ? –
                              Ecrire pour se mettre à nu...

Traduction française: V. Morillon.

142

* * *

Je vois le visage grimacant
De nouveau dans une lumière rougeâtre
Je chante la chanson finale
Et pleure : Partez !
Mes pertes attendent
Et essaient de hair
Tous mes faux passés
Pour ne choisir que le demier.
Je vois le Stop
Et en appelle à l'Espoir,
Mais Sa réponse
Est brève : Tu meurs.

Traduction française: V. Morillon.

* * *

Mon âme,
La douleur te rend transparente,
Tu voici soudain penchée
Au-dessus du gouffre des années –
Elle dorn
Légèrement.
L'infernal festin
Des dettes
Hurle.
Nu,
Il me pourrit en profondeur.
Oh! Non! Non!
Je n'ai pas vaincu
Et je n'ai pas trahi
La signification mensongère
Se déverse sur les motifs,
Elle se moque
Des misérables
"Trendre est la nuit".
Je camouflai
De nouveau mes larmes,
Glacé par le pouvoir
D'anticipation
Je l'ai consumé
A l'aide des rayons des Profondeurs.
Oh! Oui! Oui!
Refusant, j'attendais ...

Traduction française: V. Morillon.

144

* * *

Oh, Corps! –
Tu symbolises le bouclier incertain
Conue les anaques impitoyables de la vie. Mon
Ame est écoeurée par la Naiveté:
                    le SIDA des profondeurs
N'aspirera pas totalement toutes aspirations
Et érigera la pierre tombale du Reproche.
Oh, Sens qui réclamez des Mensonges
Ne voilez pas la nudité du motif
De votre anonymat. Quand vous comprendrez
Que vous avez pris le vol régulier,
Le Destin en riant te menace
Une fois de plus de famine.
Sois distant et sépare l'éphémère
De l'exigence et de la passion utilitaire,
Ne t'égare pas, lorsque tu appréhenderas
Le gué du royaume de l'Illusion,
Pare le dôme du Paradis
De tous les sacrifices possibles
Afin de les fondre à l'infondable Bonheur.

Traduction française: V. Morillon.

BIENTOT

Il y aura bientôt la guerre ! –
Je peine à respirer contre l'oreiller poussièreux.
Les graines du Mensonge –
Poursuivent leur explosion atomique.
Le pays de la misère,
S'étouffe une fois encore avec le sperme de la mémoire,
Il devra prier pour apprendre
Lorsque sera crevé l'abcès.
Il y aura bientôt la guerre ! –
La Naiveté aveugle les Perversions.
Il est impossible de capturer
Les renouveaux dans les rets du bonheur.
Il est impossible de disperser
En un éclair le bal infini des significations.
Il y aura bientôt la guerre ! –
Effondrement de l'honneur et souffrance...
Il y a un raid de nouvelles insignifications...

Traduction française: V. Morillon.

146

* * *

Je séparerai la haine du chagrin,
Je serai prisonnier du carillon
Des années perdues –
Qui a besoin
Du gémissement de la pauvreté,
Si il a érodé sa mémoire ?
J'enfonce en moi
Un regard fatigué,
J'accuse mes profondeurs –
Quelle force me caressera
Et me redonnera vie de nouveau.
Momentanément emprisonné
Dans la tombe des instants –
Ils languissent,
Ils vivent
En ceux qui croient
Que le premier et le demier moment
N'étaient destinés qu'à eux.

Traduction française: V. Morillon.

MESURE

Notre temps
Est mesuré
Par nos songes,
Par nos bienvenus –
Jaillisants de fougue première, les rêves
Sont débordements avec les cruautés
                  fanatiques des âmes.

Les délices
S'endorment au loin,
Avec l'obscurité,
Ils passent
L'éspace de temps
Dans l'absence.

Le hurlement de douleur germe au travers
                  des offenses –
Unique besoin jusqu'à la mort

L'indifference
Pour justifier
Les infidelities
Personne

Sur le mur de la haute attention
La plus interminable des vanités béates.
Vous n'obtenez que dettes sur les dettes.

148

La perversion
Hors de toute chaleur
Vivant de sensibilité
Une vision de naiveté
Qui s'évaouit

Dans la folle folie déchirant les mots.
Ils vivent en moi, sans matière,
                    tant ils me brûlent.

Traduction française: Paul Cariage.

ICÔNE

Yeux transparents
Larmes affectées
Me poussent au fond de mon âme
Plus fort que mon destin.
Et il n'y a plus rien ãdire –
Les métamorphoses me brûlent
Brodant les appels
Afin de me libérer.
L'obstination du néant,
Les distances deviennent aveugles
Caressent les fleurs fânées
Les entourant de rêves nébuleux.
Je porte les feuilles du délice,
Je colorie l'échafaud menteur
Dans la couleur originelle
Pour me figer comme un fou.
Défigurant le motif
Je colle mes plaintes dans les vers,
Par des mots insatiables.
Avec la souffrance des années
Naît le désir d'avoir des roses.
Mon corps décomposé, je reste
Vivant, tel un squelette
De dettes rongées
Qui n'existent plus.
Surmontant la nuit
J'arrive dans la lumière
Et je dépose pour eux une bougie
Accrochée à ma main.
Icône. Eux: mon fils

Et ma fille – volés
Par le quodien,
Un paysage,
Des arbres...
Et la lumière...

Traduction française: Caroline Aeby.

AU LIEU

Au lieu d'elle
Je me suis mêlé en eux –
Mon amour et mon mot,
L'antienne de mon âme.

Au lieu d'avoir
Fini de vivre –
Personne ne brille
Dans la foule en cendres.

Au lieu de chant –
Je pleure la Fin
Et prie: «au revoir»
Ma terre intérieure.

Au lieu de mort –
J'attends d'autres rôles
Pour jouer les meilleurs
Sans buts gardés.

Traduction: Chris Bernard

FACE

Je vois la face souriante
En lumière encore rousse,
Je chante le chant final
Et je crie: Fuyez!

Je ne sens plus mon poids
Et tente de haîr
Tous mes fqux dépassements
Pour saisir l'ultime.

Je vois l'arret,
Et j'appelle l'espoir,
Mais il se retire,
Rapetisse: Vous mourez.

Traduction: Paul Cariage

153

* * *

Brûler la vie
C'est fouler la lumière
Dans son étreinte,
Jeter au feu
Les années déjà passées
Leurs restes douloureux arrachés
A l'âme mutilée.
Oh ! Ihn !
La douce Naiveté et l'aveuglement
Ne feront pas écho aux appels:
Il y a l'archer du Temps –
Qui, lorsqu'il frappe, vous donne encore plus.
Depuis si longtemps ce désir
De hurler : "Oui !"
En direction de la fétide
Fosse aux rêves.
Brûle maintenant –
Cela n'a plus d'importance –
Je supporterai vaillament
Les souvenirs qui s'éclipsent,
Je suis épuisé...
Je suis blanchi par les années...
Je me dissous...

Traduction française: V. Morillon.

SUPERMANIFOLD

La condamnation est éparpillée
Par la neige des idylles –
Arriverai – je ã sauver ma Lumiére,
Pourrais – je remplir le vide
De mon ultime souci
Avec la boue et les etcaeteras ? –
Non!
Svastika de rêves non-dits
Caresses –
Empoisonnées par la raison.
Supermanifold
De la vie
Ment
Dans son délire...

Traduction française: Caroline Aeby.

Poems in German

POEPHYSICS

Poesie, eine Supernova der Gefühle. Physik, eine Supernova der Ideen. Eine neue Zeichenfolge von Buchstaben, eine neue Reihe von mathematischen Symbolen sind die zwei Seiten des Mondes, ein Außerirdischer binär. Hinter meiner Seele bilden sie eine Sphinx. Ich trenne nicht die Ideen der Physik und die Metaphern der Poesie. Die unkontrollierbare kalte Fusion benötigt mein Herz um sie zu erschaffen. Je neuere der Kraftstoff desto weiter wird der Schuss in die Zukunft sein.

Ich glaube Poesie kann nicht wie eine Formel konstruiert werden. Äußere Regeln sind transparent für sie, und nur diejenigen. Die von innen kommen erwecken sie zum Leben. Die einzige wahre Regel ist: Ohne eine kritische Masse wird die Reaktion der Kreativität nicht gestartet. Die Dichte der Gefühle und Ideen wird so groß , dass unabhängig von meinen Begierden es eine Explosion in die Unendlichkeit geben wird.

Sie werden alles durchdringen. Ich bin einfach nicht in der Lage, sie zu vermeiden, und ich n habe keine Angst, dass sich jemand über meine Schwächen , Leiden , Komplexe , meine Nachteile Lustig macht.

Poephysics erhebt mich über sie zu erheben, über die Lebensart, über die Zeit.

Übersetzung: Peter Mahnke

SEMI

Semiwahrheit, Semigewissen,
Semimeinungsstreit und Semialltag,
Semiwelt? – Die sind das Schicksal nicht wert.
Semigedächtnis? – Weg damit! –
Ich habe vergessen.
Das Abführmittel der Seelen, die "Semi"
Unterspült den Kreis der Sinne –
Der Semifeind mit dem Semivorwurf
Semilügt, daß er Semifreund ist.
Der Handel mit den Semigefühlen,
Die Speise ist das Semifabrikat.
Der Semimann-Semibruder
Ist semisatt von der Semiliebe.
Die Semimacht ist die Semifreiheit,
Alle schämen sich – alle schweigen.
Freuen sich über die Semifürsorge,
Semischlafen wir – vielleicht wieder zurück?...

Übersetzung: Steven Duplij

ZEILE

Du bist – meine Zeile,
Eine Handvoll von Symbolen.
Du bist – die Wand i n das "Nicht-Ich",
Wieder – verzeih mir.
Mit den Bytes die Files von Träumen
Brechen aus ins Delirium
Unterbrochen durch das Stöhnen
Derjenigen, die nicht da sind.
Aufschreiend lese ich
Die Träne ihrer Verzweiflung,
Ich warte ab, bis die Gewitter
Des Zwischenleidens aufhören.
Auf den Bildschirm in das Nichts
Lege ich mein Kruzifix,
Ich stelle den Handel
Mit Grundsätzlichem ein,
Den Text stelle ich um.
Du bist – meine Zeile,
Eine Handvoll von Symbolen.
Du bist – die Wand in das "Nicht-Ich",
Wieder – verzeih mir...

Übersetzung: Steven Duplij

ICH HABE ES NICHT BEMERKT

Das Alter habe ich nicht bemerkt –
Niemand fragt nach mir,
Niemand ruft mich an.
Meine Kinder führen ihre eigenen
In den Kindergarten.
Ich bin müde zu rennen,
Aber man kann mit der Leere
Das Gedächtnis nicht löschen.
Es gibt keine Geschehen – mit den Jahren
Verschwinden die Seelenschmerzen.
Ich habe mich mit Vergangenheit überschüttet,
Aber die Schmerzen wurden gestillt nicht:
Die Ewigkeit meiner Nächte...
Die Kälte meines Bettes...

Übersetzung: Steven Duplij

FENSTER

Erwachend... in ihrem fremden Bett...
Bin ich krank und betrunken,
Und voller verrückter
Emotionen, Gefühle
Und Erinnerungen...
Gott ! Verzeih mir –
Befreie mich
Von der hässlichen Einsamkeit
Und dem Stein (der Last)
Von dem entblößten Vorwurf weniger
Dann stöhnen.
Ich habe in Trance Fenster gesehen
In die Dunkelheit –
Sein Wind begrub
das letzte Zeichen der Seele...

Übersetzung: Peter Mahnke

IKONE

Durchsichtige Augen,
Gekünstelte Tränen
Rufen zum Grund der Seele
Stärker als das Schicksal.
Und – nichts mehr zu sagen,
Metamorphosen verbrennen mich,
Besticken die Berufung,
Um den Sklaven mit ihnen zu sühnen.
Das störrische Nichts,
Verblendete Fernen
Liebkosen mit der Gischt meiner Träume
Die toten Blumen.
Ich verschanze mich
Hinter dem Laub der Wonnen,
Ich färbe das Schafott der Lüge
Mit dem Ursprung – ich bin bereit
In Wahnsinn zu gefrieren.
Verstümmelnd die Melodie,
Klebe ich das Stöhnen mit Strophen
Von unersättlichen Worten zu,
Ich begreife mit dem Schmerz
Meiner Jahre den Rosenwunsch.
Verwest bleibe ich als Skelett
Am Leben, von Pflichten zernagt,
Welche schon verschwunden sind.
Die Nacht bezwingend,
Gehe ich für einen Augenblick
In die Offenheit,

Ich stelle für sie die Kerze auf,
Angewachsen an meine Hand.
Die Ikone – mein Sohn,
Meine Tochter, gestohlen
Durch den Alltag,
Die Landschaft,
Einige Bäume...
Und Licht...

Übersetzung: Steven Duplij

TRAUM

Mir träumt von der Nacht –
Die Gärten mit den Gräbern.
Zwei Schritte – weg
Die Schuld meiner Seele.
Herausreißen sein Stöhnen,
Der Nimbus ist getaut.
Halt an!
Das Leben – Zyclotron.
Ich flehe: lesen Sie
Gehen Sie nicht ab,
Versteckend Ihr Antlitz,
Zurufend den Augenblick.
Überfluten mit Träumen
Die Meinung verfaulend
Zu sein die Asche
Als Gabe zum Los.
Entschuldigung für Abbruch,
Für Null, für Handel.
Ohne Sinn für sie,
Für mich Haus, Arbeit,
Leichenhalle.
Ich bin aufgestanden –
Der Strahl gleitet
Am Grundsätzlichen
Des Wahnsinns:
Ich drehe den Auf ruhr
Des Innersten ab.
Naivität nagt, verwundet, rächt.
Meine Sünde ist entthront – AIDS der Gipfel.

Übersetzung: Steven Duplij

FALSCHER TRAUM

Am nächsten Morgen sehe ich
            den falschen Traum:
Ich bin in der Vergangenheit, verliebt,
Liebste – lebendig.
Folternder Geruch der unsanften Hände,
Das Fest der gewöhnlichen Laster.
Plötzliches Klopfen:
Sie kam ohne Genehmigung.
Schluchzend.
Das Schicksal betete kreischend –
            als man sollte. Fieber.

Die Zweige der schrecklichen Hoffnung
      faulten hinter dem Fenster Geteilt durch
            den Abgrund der Verluste,
Ich akzeptiere den Abbruch,
Aber nur das Spielen von oben herab,
lachen richtet den jungfräulichen
Schmerz auf mich aus.

Am nächsten Morgen sehe ich
            den falsche Traum :
Ich bin in der Vergangenheit, verliebt,
Liebste – am Leben ...

Übersetzung: Peter Mahnke

PASSAGIER

Ich bin nur ein lustiger Passagier
Von dem Nirgendwo vorbeifahrenden Zug,
Hält bei kalten Wohnungen
Und ergebnislosen Suchen
        welche mich erschöpften.
Vergessen, humorvoll, ängstlich
Ich erwärme nicht das Fenster mit dem Atem.

Kein Ende für lästige anstrengende Straßenrändern –
Es ist das Ende der Unvermeidbarkeit .
Schlafende Erde –
Ist ein geduldiger Friedhof Drohend mit Axt-Kreuzen,
Scharfe glitzernde Krallen des Bösen
Zerdrücken meine Seele in vergeblichem Geschrei.

Vom der Hoffnungen verlassen
        für den Augenblick des Windstoßes,
Bereits niemand liebkost meinen Schmerz,
In meinen Augen spiegelt
        es weiß wie hinter Scheuklappen,
Es sind die endlose Qualen des Lebens.

Übersetzung: Peter Mahnke

VERGANGENES

Blätter – von Blättern
Überdeckt.
Leben – über ihnen
Schmelzend.
Halt, Spiegelbild! –
Denn ich lebe.
Blätter – von Blättern
Überdeckt.

Zärtlichkeit – die Trennung
Bejahend.
Sünde – gewinnt
Triumphierend.
Dann Erschießung durch den Augenblick –
Verberge dein Ganzes.
Zärtlichkeit – die Trennung
Bejahend.

Vergangenes – aufgegeben
Im Heute.
Übelkeit –
Noch lärmender Gelage.
Die Welt in Gelächter pervertiert –
Heuchler, sie.
Vergangenes – aufgegeben
Im Heute.

Übersetzung: Volker Knecht

SUPERMANIFOLD

Verlust wird mit Schnee der Idylle bedeckt –
Ob mein Licht zu retten ist,
Ob meine letzte Besorgung
Mit Jauche der Pünktchen zuzukleben ist? –
Nein!
Das Hakenkreuz von unerfüllten Träumen,
Liebkosungen –
Werden die Vernunft vergiften.
Supermanifold
Vom Leben
Lügt
Im Delirium...

Übersetzung: Steven Duplij

DIE HALBE STUNDE

Wieder fahre ich mit Dir in der gleichen Straßenbahn. Auch heute. Gestern. Jeden Tag. Diese halbe Stunde. Sie gibt mir Leben und Ertragen für die restlichen 23 1/2 Stunden des Tages. Dein beharrlicher und kecker Blick. Dein scheinbar wichtiges Geschwätz mit der Bekannten. Irgendwas willst Du beweisen. Du sprichst fast immer allein. Auch mit jedem Kopfnicken, jedem Bewegen Deiner schwarzen tiefen Augen: das gleiche. Ich weiß, daß Du mich spürst, daß wir uns wahrnehmen. Ohne gemeinsame Sprache. Ohne gemeinsame Kultur. Wir wissen einfach, daß wir beieinander sind. Diese halben Stunden. Du trägst Deine Hakennase mit Stolz. Wenn ich schaue, wendest Du Dich ab, aber nicht ganz. Läßt Deinen Blick über die anderen schweifen. Und von neuem erwartest Du und forderst meinen Blick heraus. Ja, ich kann mich nicht losreißen. Das gehört sich zwar nicht, das weiß ich. Aber was soll ich tun mit meinem Streben zu Dir? Schon seit längerem habe ich mir versprochen, keine Frau mehr zu beachten, mich nicht an sie zu verausgaben. Wieviele leere Worte gab es schon, ja... nach allem, was mit mir gechehen ist. Mit den Frauen. Mit mir. In meinem Leben so viele von ihnen, so viel Verrat und Demütigungen, daß es scheint, ich sollte damit endlich aufhören. Jedoch nein, immer wieder von neuem schau ich mit Zittern hinein in diesen Abgrund – die weibliche Seele – immer neue Schläge erhaltend. Wohin wird das alles führen? Ich weiß es nicht. Aber ich ahne es. Genau wieder so. Wieder zu einem Fiasko? Kann sein. Das würde ich nicht wollen. Die Hoffnung, wie ein ewiger grüner Baum, wächst zum wiederholten mal heraus aus den abgebrannten Resten der vorausgegangen Lieben, als ob es diese nie gegeben hätte.

171

Ich fühle, daß Du einsam bist. Wie ich. Ja, Du hast einen Sohn. Du hast eine Deine Arbeit gern, wenn auch nicht zu sehr. Viele Freunde. Nur Frauen. Vielleicht einen Liebhaber. Aber keinen großen und bedeutenden. Den gibt es nicht. Alles liegt in der Vergangenheit... lediglich Bruchstücke sind noch da. Diese unerfüllbaren, immer wiederkehrenden Ver-sprechungen, die wir so hassen. Und dieseble dumpfe Erwartung, die wir bis zum Kniezittern spüren. Warten auf was? Oder auf wen? Wir beide wissen die Antwort. Wenn sich unbemerkt von den anderen unsere Blicke berühren. Wenn ich an der Haltestelle den Zigarettenrauch, der in Deiner Brust war, einatme. Oh, wie ich ihn beneide!

Jeden Tage versuche ich, mit dir zu sprechen, versuche ich, irgendeinen Vorwand zu finden. Und so auch heute. Fast hätte ich Dich gegrüßt. Du kamst zur Haltestelle speziell auf meine Seite. Da sah ich, Du hattest die Wahl. Ich bemerkte, Du wartest auch. So wie ich. Aber im letzten Moment diese unmenschliche Anstrengung – von neuem und zum wievelten mal – tun wir so als blieben wir uns fremd. Welcher Unsinn!

Das war's. Die Straßenbahn erreicht das Zentrum. Meine Haltestelle. Ich gehe einen halben Meter an Dir vorbei. Deine Anspannung fühlend in diesem Augenblick. Und auch ich bin angespanntbis zum Verrücktwerden. Wir verabschieden uns mit Blicken. Unbemerkt von den anderen. Hoffend auf unser Morgen. Geduldig. Wissend, daß sich alles wiederholt. Unser unsichtbares Berührungsspiel. Unsere endlose halbe Stunde.

Aber nein. Du hast Dich geirrt. Sie wird sich nicht mehr wiederholen. Unser gemeinsamer Augenblick – der letzte. Morgen fliege ich ab in ein anderes Land, in eine andere Welt – zu anderen Frauen. Damit ich Dich lieben kann – in ihnen...

Überzetzung: Wolfram und Edda von Oertzen

Poems in Italian

POEPHYSICS

Poesia, una supernova di sentimenti. Fisica, una supernova di idee. Un nuovo elenco di lettere, un nuovo elenco di simboli matematici sono le due facce della Luna, un binario alieno. Dietro la mia anima formano una sfinge. Io non separo le idee della fisica e le metafore della poesia. L'incontrollabile fusione fredda è necessaria al mio cuore per crearle. Più nuovo è il combustibile e più lontano sara' l'impatto nel futuro.

Credo che la Poesia non possa essere costruita come una formula. Per Lei le Regole esterne sono trasparenti, e solo quelle interne vive. Una sola regola è vera: senza una massa critica la reazione della Creatività non si avviera'. I sentimenti e le idee sono collassati ad una densita' cosi alta che, indipendentemente dal mio desiderio c'è un'esplosione nell'Infinito.

Sono tutti penetranti. Semplicemente Io non sono in grado di evitarli, e non ho più paura che qualcuno sorrida della mia debolezza, delle mie pene, dei miei complessi e dei miei svantaggi.

La Poephysics mi permette di elevarmi su di loro, sul modo di vivere, nel corso del tempo.

Traduzione: Roberto Casalbuoni

ALIEN

Io non sono un estraneo –
Io sono – un uomo,
Amore – cambiamenti interiori ,
Avere – quello che posso.
Io non sono un alieno
Tra ricordi –
Ricerca di ortografia
Di tentativi supremi.
Intrecciando gli spazi
Di bugie diverse,
Mi sciolgo in tracce
Di dolore – per non morire...

Traduzione: Roberto Casalbuoni

ESPIAZIONE INFINITA

In quel mondo,
Come sul bordo di una lama,
Sto catturando l' aria dell'anima.
Sorridere, sono stato cresciuto
nelle perdite.
Che cosa è rimasto per me? – Scrivere .
Cosa scrivere , quando il tempo appiccicoso
È percepito dopo la sua scomparsa.
Abbandonato da loro in con scarse possibilita'.
La mia riflessione – scheletro appassito.
Sto facendo il mio letto per due
Perche' essi non appaiano da La.
Fino al mattino io salvo il mio calore
Perché , essere né questi né quelli.
A quel tempo, impazzendo di paura ,
Con l' infinito io macchio la mia carta .
Forse, questa è la loro espiazione:
Io brindo a tutto quello che diviene freddo
Sul fondo.
In quel mondo,
Come sul bordo di una lama...

Traduzione: Roberto Casalbuoni

NOI E LORO

Il mio amore, il tuo amore
Considerati come continuazioni
Sono stati, ormai, uccisi.
Da chi? –
da noi
E da loro.
Sono roso, sei roso
Dalla solitudine e dall' ispirazione
Dei nostri sentimenti strappati.
Da chi? –
Da loro
E da noi.
Cerchiamo di ridere,
Per salutare la Stazione Liberta'
che sta fondendosi nel miraggio piangente.
Di chi la colpa ? –
Nostra
E loro.
Abbiamo pensato abbastanza
Per chiudere le pagine
Della nostra insensata costruzione della
storia.
Per chi? –
per loro
E per noi.

Traduzione: Roberto Casalbuoni

UN NUOVO ANNO MOLTO "FELICE"

Città – è morto,
Le persone – sono ubriache .
L'anima – è triste,
La vita – era spazzatura.
La pioggia ha perso le sue lacrime,
Il cervello ha perso la sua mente .
Frontiere vuote
Fuori binari.
Cuore – come in falso,
Scopo – come in un errato.
Senso profondo – nel nulla:
Dio dice : "Vattene!"...

Traduzione: Roberto Casalbuoni

ANGELO

Non essere triste, mio Angelo del Male:
Non tutto è passato –
                 il gemito, la passione.
La mia anima stanca stava abbracciando
Con anelito
                       sulla tomba ferita.
Non alzare ponti sulla volta
Di tutti gli avvincenti legami –
La perdita delle radici e degli anni
                senza senso e delle parole inutili.
Falli pregare per la felicità,
Non diffamarti nella sporcizia.
Il destino ha emesso il suo verdetto prostrato
         sui miei polsi e beffandomi nuovamente.
E – il rendezvous con un motivo pazzo
Sta cessando. Bussando alla notte,
               rigettando gruppi di scuse
Ingenuo, mi adeguero' alle loro regole.

Traduzione: Roberto Casalbuoni

SOGNO SBAGLIATO

La mattina dopo vedo
                 il sogno sbagliato:
Io sono nel passato, innamorato,
Il piu' caro – vivo.
Odore torturatore di mani scortesi,
La festa dei vizi abituali.
Bussare – improvvisamente:
Lei è venuta senza permesso .
Singhiozzando.
Il destino invocato
Come si dovrebbe. Febbre.
I rami di terribile Speranza marcita
dietro la finestra
                 squarciata da abissi di perdite,
Accetto la distruzione,
Ma solo come un gioco dall'alto,
                                 ridendo
Convertendo il dolore-fanciullo
                          alla mia linea.
Il mattino dopo vedo
                 il sogno sbagliato:
Io sono nel passato, innamorato,
Il piu' caro – vivo...

Traduzione: Roberto Casalbuoni

BLITZ

Al di là delle persiane della mia giovinezza – i miei anni
Rifondere il Nulla
Con la svastica delle gioie supreme per illuminare
Il tutto con la creazione di carestie.
La luce glassa le linee dipinte
        ancora con atto dolente
           del Gioco "Perdonami" –
Agli altri – parti Io porgero'.
Il sogno del passato si diffonde
Dietro le mie colpevoli finestre –
Io sarò sul bordo per chiuderle:
Un passo – e il volo e' impedito.
Il chiuso anello della depressione
        rotola il destino verso il basso.
La confessione spruzza in silenzio
Con gli incartamenti dei miei anni schiacciati.
No, io non cado in ginocchio,
Io non faccio cadere il motivo.
Ultima scommessa con la mia vita come un Blitz,
Modulazione di figure morte.

Traduzione: Roberto Casalbuoni

VOLUME

Ho pensato invano –
Il tempo è mio, senza fretta .
Un sogno sciocco –
Mio volume pieno di vita.
Sto diventando muto
Abbracciando infine una manciata di pagine
Non lette e con scritto:
"A dopo".
Tutti gli impeti saranno superati,
esposti in mura di volumi alieni,
Marci dimenticandosi del Dentro
Reintrecciando il refrain dei sogni dormienti.
Io lo avvicinero'
sorridendo dal dolore, soccombendo,
Aspettando parole finali
    nella festa brutale delle idee vuote
E degli dei avvelenati...

Traduzione: Roberto Casalbuoni

SETACCIO

Sfogliando le pagine di strade divise
Di corpi deformati di città aliene ,
Ho chiesto all'ombra turbinante su di loro
quando i sogni si realizzano.
Il significato coperto
Taglia l'incontro
Con i colpi dei ladri
E le frustate degli dei:
Poi il volo – setaccio di separazioni
Setaccia il resto
Di parole prive di senso.
Io accarrezzo il disegno di trasformarle in tenerezza
Con gesti banali
Di giorni educati
Non vivendo sulla negligenza
Di vuoti non-testi
Per un lungo tempo ,
Più aspro della morte .

Traduzione: Roberto Casalbuoni

IL PROSSIMO FALSO ANNO

L'anno – passato ,
La vita – rifiutata.
Io piango – vattene !
La risposta – "gioiosa".
Ho bisogno – di essere ,
Ma il destino – cosi come è,
Come ape che punge
Bacio perverso.
Richiamare è morto ,
Tutti i colori – grigio.
Desideri – diffusione,
Tutti gli amici – lontani.
Loro amano – in vendita,
Diventano tornello.
Io porto una vela :
Ultimo colpo – un sorriso.
La patria – bugie:
'Tutto passa'
La libertà – muore,
Il falso futuro – erba...

Traduzione: Roberto Casalbuoni

SEMI...

Semiverita' e semicoscienza ,
Semiargomento e semivita.
Semimondo? – Non e' un destino che valga.
Semimemoria? – Vattene! – Ho dimenticato.
Come una purga per le anime ,
"Semi – "scioglie il cerchio del significato –
Con un semirimprovero un seminemico
Sta mentendo che e' un semiamico .
La vendita con semisentimenti,
Il cibo è semilavorato.
Semimarito – semifratello
È semipieno di semiamore.
Semipotenza è semiliberta',
Tutti si vergognano
E non denunciano
Gioia seminteressata
Noi siamo semiaddormentati –
Indietro nuovamente?

Traduzione: Roberto Casalbuoni

NUCLEO

La serata strisciante –
Sono stanco di anni ,
Spostare le sguardo addolorato
Dalla carta da parati alla ghirlanda
Di gioie perdute
Il mio sogno e' decaduto come un nucleo
Primordiale da futili mie parti.
Non ci sono eventi –
Io porto le tentazioni
Alla loro tomba:
La mia anima – singhiozza violentemente e mani
– Nel sangue .
Io sfoglio nella notte. E i suoi miasmi
Rubano dentro di me
Per imputridire la vergogna di sforzi morti .
Essere ingrassato con il successo ,
Ingenuita' addormentata,
Che rompe le prognosi
Con il ricordo dei giorni perduti:
Il volo si e' bloccato
Nel punto più alto, ridendo
Dello pseudosignificato dei passati
Per cadere più dolorosamente .

Traduzione: Roberto Casalbuoni

FINESTRA

Risveglio... Il suo letto alieno...
Sono sofferente e ubriaco,
E pieno di pazze
Emozioni, sentimenti
Ricordi...
Mio signore! Perdonami –
Liberami
Dalla orrenda solitudine
E la pietra
Di nudo rimprovero meno
Che di lamenti
Ho visto finestre di rapimento
Nel buio –
Il suo vento stava seppellendo
L'ultimo marchio dell'anima...

Traduzione: Roberto Casalbuoni

PASSEGGERO

Sono solo un buffo passeggero
Del treno che non passa da nessuna parte,
Soste in freddi appartamenti
E ricerche infruttuose
Mi hanno esaurito.
Dimenticato, divertente, ansioso
Non riscaldo la finestra con il respiro.
Nessuna fine a noiosi stancanti cigli delle strade
E' il fondo della inevitabilità .
La terra dormiente – è il paziente cimitero
Minacciare con l'ascia,
Affilate e e minacciose zampe luccicanti
Schiacciare la mia anima in inutili lamenti.
Le speranze sono lievito
Per il vento del momento,
Già nessuno accarezza il mio dolore,
Nei miei occhi come dietro bianche persiane,
C'è una infinita angoscia di vita.

Traduzione: Roberto Casalbuoni

QUELLO CHE E' PASSATO

Foglie – sono coperte
Con altre foglie.
Le vite – sono fuse
Su di loro.
Riflessione – ferma!
Io sono vivo .
Foglie – sono coperte
Con altre foglie .
Tenerezza – prende il sopravvento
Il suo addio .
Peccato – supera
L'esultanza.
Per essere colpito dall' istante –
Nascondi il tuo fato.
Tenerezza – prende il sopravvento
Il suo addio .
Quello che e' passato – lascia
La sua strada oggi .
Malattia –
Di tavole incompiute .
Mondo pervertito in risate –
Loro ipocriti.
Quello che e' passato lascia
La sua strada oggi

Traduzione: Roberto Casalbuoni

IN UN SOFFIO DI VITA

Sì, ho conosciuto
Cio' che non lascero' senza scopo –
Il sogno del momento è pieno di delicatezza, di male .
Le braccia del fato, i suoi occhi – quasi vivi –
Non mi permettono di cantare le parole della follia.
Sto aprendo una nebulosa di gas per l'ultimo,
Non rovente e desiderabile istante:
Sono dentro un soffio di vita –
La chiamata nella mia stanza d'ingresso
È rimandare l'esecuzione per un'ora.
C'è la stessa deserta serata di gomma:
Cosa da' quest'ora,
Quanti anni ha rubato?
Nel caso in cui tu non abbia motivi
                    per amare e piangere
Lascia il tuo sonetto esaurirsi
                    ripetendosi.

Traduzione: Roberto Casalbuoni

SUPERMANIFOLD

Il destino è coperto
Con la neve degli idilli –
Sia per salvare la mia luce
Che per vestire
Le miei ultime ed interne preoccupazioni
Nel fango degli eccetera? No!
Svastica dei sogni
Non detti e inespressi ,
Carezze – avvelenate dalla mente .
Il supermanifold della vita sta
In parole senza senso ...

Traduzione: Roberto Casalbuoni

Poems in Spanish

POEFÍSICA

La poesía, una supernova de sentimentos. La física, una supernova de ideas. Una nueva cadena de letras, una nueva cadena de símbolos matemáticos son las dos caras de la Luna, un binario extraño. Por detrás de mi alma forman una esfinge. No separo las ideas de la Física y las metáforas de la Poesía. La fusión fría incontrolable es necesaria para que mi corazón las crea. Cuanto más nuevo el combustible más lejos irá el tiro hasia el Futuro.

Creo que la Poesiá no se puede construir como fórmula. Las normas externas son transparantes para Ella, y sólo las internas están vivas. Sólo una norma es cierta: sin una masa crítica no se iniciará la reacción de la Creatividad. Los sentimentos y las ideas se comprimen hasta densidades tan grandes que, con independensia de mi deceo, hay una explosión hasia el Infinito.

Lo penetran todo. Sencillamente, no soy capaz de evitarlos, y ya no tengo miedo de que alguien se estÂ riendo de mi debelidad, mis sufrimientos, mis complejos, mis aspectos negativos.

La Poefísica me permite elevar por encima de ellos, por encima del estilo de vida, por encima del Tiempo.

Tradujo el Trudi Kiebala

195

LLAMADO AL PASADO

No llamen al pasado
Allí sólo hay inmóviles estatuas de sentimientos
No llamen al pasado
Allí sólo tiemblan párpados de requerdos – en
crujido.
Que nada bueno
Espere en la libertad del sueño:
La cuidada fachada de mentiras
Se llevará por un instante la mirada desde el fondo.
La peluca gastada de los años
Pincha con agujas de los días los ojos:
No llamen al pasado
Para descubrir la cruz del futuro.

Tradujo al castellano el Miguel Krshjschanows

EL EXTRAÑO

No soy forastero –
Soy – un hombre,
El amor – cambios internos,
Tengo – loque puedo.
No soy un extraño
Entre los recuerdos –
Buscando la ortografia
De intentos supremos.
Retorciendo los espacios
De distitas mentiras,
Me derrito en huellas
De dolor – para no morir.

Tradujo el Trudi Kiebala

CRIBA

Volviendo las páginas de las calles divididas
De los cuerpos deformados de ciudades extrañas,
Le pregunté a las Sombras por encima de sus remolinos
De dónde proviene la ejecución de los sueños.

El sentido salpicado corta la reunión
Con golpes de mendigos y azotes de dioses:
Luego la huida – la criba de las despedidas
Tamizará lo que queda de las palabras sin sendido.

Aliso el diseño de transmutar en ternura
Con gestos manidos de días amanerados
Sin vivir mucho tiempo de la negligencia.
De los subtextos vacíos, lo cual es más duro que la
muerte.

Tradujo el Trudi Kiebala

EXPIACION INFINITA

En ese mundo,
Como en el filo de una navaja,
Una vez más trato de agarrar el aire del Alma.
Sonriente, me han criado las pérdidas.
¿Qué me ha quedado? – Escribir.

¿Qué debería escribir, cuando el Tiempo pegajoso
Se conoce tras su desaparición.
Por si acaso me abandonan todos,
Mi reflejo es un esqueleto marchitado.

Hago mi cama para dos,
Para que ellos, en mi sueño, no aparezcan de allí.
Hasta la mañana guardo mi calor para nada.
¿Para qué?, no serán ni éstos ni aquéllos.

En ese momento, enloqueciendo de miedo,
Mancharé mi papel con el infinito.
Quizá sea ésta su contrición:
Beberé todo lo que se enfría
En el Fondo.

En ese Mundo,
Como en el filo de la navaja...

Tradujo el Trudi Kiebala

UN AÑO NUEVO MUY "FELIZ"

La ciudad – está muerta,
La gente – está borracha .
El alma – está triste,
La vida – era un desperdicio.
La lluvia perdió sus lágrimas ,
El cerebro perdió la cordura.
Fronteras vacías
Fuera de línea .
Corazón – como en falso,
Meta – como equivocada.
Sentido profundo – vacío:
Dios dice : "¡Que se valla!"...

Tradujo el Pedro Alvarez

ÁNGEL

No estés triste, mi Ángel malvado:
No todo se ha ido –
       el lamento, la pasión.
Mi alma cansada se cobijaba
Con el anhelo
       en el cementerio herido.
No levanten lazos en la bóveda
De todos los vendajes de absorción –
El malgasto de disparos y sinsentido
De los años perdidos y palabras inútiles.
Hacedlos que oren por la felicidad,
No difames a ti mismo suciamente.
El Destino ha dado un veredicto mintiendo
Sobre mis muñecas y se mofa de nuevo.
Y – el encuentro con motivo de locura
Está cesando. Llamando a la Noche,
Excretando un cúmulo de excusas
Ingenuo, me quedo con el dominio de ellas.

Tradujo el Pedro Alvarez

SUEÑO INCORRECTO

A la mañana siguiente veo
              el sueño incorrecto:
Estoy en el pasado, me enamoro,
         mis seres queridos – con vida.
Olor de manos que tortura no gentilmente,
La fiesta de los vicios habituales.
Golpea la puerta – de repente:
Ella llegó sin permiso.
Sollozando.
El destino oró gritando –
            como uno debe. Fiebre.
Las ramas de la terrible Esperanza se pudren
            detrás de la ventana
Se separan con un abismo de pérdidas,
Yo acepto la demolición,
Pero sólo como jugando desde arriba,
            riendo
Convirtiendo la doncella dolor
          en mi línea.
A la mañana siguiente veo
El sueño incorrecto:
Estoy en el pasado, me enamoro,
Mis seres queridos – con vida...

Tradujo el Pedro Alvarez

Poems in Portuguese

REFLEXÕES

Expulso meu ódio
Em uma cesta de paixão -
Sua estranha devoção
É um vexame na noite
De pseudo-felicidade.
Escapando para um sacrifício
De vingança negligenciada,
Agarrando uma mentira, uma lisonja,
Afetada por significados,
Desmanchada por sonhos rápidos,
Cortando a miséria,
Gritando ao passar.
Aos anos roubados
Pérolas de pensamento
Reiterando momentos lívindos
De minha infância destruida,
Molestada honestamente
Com tentativas de engano,
Mas fingindo sinceridade
Esquecendo os doces momentos
De alegria interrompidos
Pelo desfile de mitos
Não essenciais.
Agora eu estou atacando
A cidade com sucessos
Sem precedentes.

Tradução por Tersinka Pereira

EM VEZ DISSO

Em vez de dar a ela
Entrego-lhes a eles
Meu amor e minha palavra
E o hino de minha alma.

Em vez de ter vivido
Pela vida afora
Sem nenhum incentivo
Construo com as cinzas
Um punhado de ilusões.

Em vez de cantar
Eu choro o fim de tudo
E rezo: "até mais tarde..."
Dentro de minha terra.

Em vez da morte
Eu espero representar
Mais papéis e fazê-lo
Como se fossem
O melhor de meus ideais.

Tradução por Tersinka Pereira

Poems in Norwegian

POESIFYSIKK

Poesi, en supernova av følelser. Fysikk, en supernova av ideer. En ny streng av bokstaver, en ny rekke med matematiske symboler er de to sidene av månen, en fremmed binær. Bak min sjel danner de en sfinks. Jeg vil ikke skille ideene om fysikk og metaforene i poesi fra hverandre. Den ukontrollerbare kalde fusjon er nødvendig for mitt hjerte for å kunne skape dem. Jo nyere drivstoffet er, jo lengre skudd inn i fremtiden blir dette.

Jeg tror poesi ikke kan sees på som en formel. Ytre regler er gjennomsiktige for henne, og kun de indre av dem er levende. Den eneste regelen som er sann er: Uten en kritisk masse vil kreativitets-reaksjonen ikke starte. Følelser og ideer er kollapset til så store tettheter at uavhengig av mine ønsker vil det være en eksplosjon til uendeligheten.

De er gjennomtrengende overalt. Jeg er ikke i stand til å unngå dem, og jeg er ikke lenger redd for at noen vil flire over min svakhet, mine lidelser, mine komplekser, mine minuser.

Poesifysikk lar meg heve meg over dem, over livets vei, over selve tiden.

Oversettelse: Iver Brevik

Poems in Serbian

ПОЕФИЗИКА

Поезија је као супернова осећања. Физика је као супернова идеја. Линија стиха и линија формуле су као две стране Месеца, као бинарна звезда ванземаљаца. У мојој души ове линије су као једна сфинга. Ја не раздвајам идеје физике и метафоре поезије. Да бисте их креирали из ничега, потребна је неконтролисана термонуклеарна фузија креативности. Што је нетривијалније гориво, то ће пуцањ бити даље у будућност.

Међутим, ја верујем да поезија не може бити исконструисана тако тачно као формула. Спољни закони и прописи су транспарентни за њу. Она живи само унутрашње, интуитивно. А њен главни закон је: без критичне масе страдања, реакција креативности не почиње. Осећања и идеје колапсирају до таквих густина да, независно од моје жеље, настаје бесконачна експлозија.

Идеје и осећања све прожимају. Немогуће их је избећи у себи. Па онда – ја се не бојим што ће се неко подсмевати мојој слабости, мојим патњама, мојим комплексима и мојим минусима...

Поефизика ми омогућава да се издигнем изнад њих и изнад свега, изнад разних потребштина, уобичајеног начина живота, изнад времена.

Translated by Branko Dragovich

СРЕЋА НА ОДСТОЈАЊУ

Каква срећа – бити далеко од њих,
Каква срећа – преживети без љубави.
Дошле су без размишљања – не.
Угледао сам у ормару – њихов скелет.
Озлојеђеност дугодишња?
Слобода? – Да.
И менторства ишчезла као вода.
И као увек –
Поново сам усамљен.
А да бих био непотребан и вама и њима –
Не треба храбрости и суза.
Данас поново мало сам порастао
И доспео у поље ништавила.
Дођи што пре,
Зар не чекам и лажем.
И себе и вас – на обали
Наивних снова.
И увек питање:
Кога има, а кога нема.
Заплетена ствар
Расплета чека...

Translated by Branko Dragovich

СУПЕРМНОГОСТРУКОСТ ЖИВОТА

Безнађе посипано
        снежном идилом –
Да ли ћу сачувати моје светло
Да ли залепити
Последњу бригу –
Обманом из тачкица? – Не!
Коло снова недоречених,
Нежности – затроване разумом.
Супермногострукост
Живота –
        у сулудост...

Translated by Branko Dragovich

Poems in Polish

POEFIZIKA

Poezja jako supernowa uczuć. Fizyka jako supernowa idei. Werset wiersza i wiersz wzoru jak dwie strony Księżyca, jak gwiazda binarna przybyszów. W mojej duszy te wiersze tworzą jedność jak Sfinks. Nie rozdzielam idei fizyki i poetyckich metafor. Żeby je stworzyć, potrzeba niekontrolowanej syntezy termojądrowej twórczości. Im bardziej niezwykłe paliwo, tym strzał sięga dalej w przyszłość.

Nie wierzę jednak, że poezja może być skonstruowana precyzyjnie jak wzór. Zewnętrzne przepisy i prawa są dla niej przezroczyste – żywe tylko wewnętrzne, intuicyjne. I główne prawo: bez krytycznej masy cierpienia reakcja tworzenia się nie rozpocznie.

Idee i uczucia są wszechogarniające. Nie da się uniknąć ich w sobie. A wtedy – nie boję się, że ktoś będzie szydził z mojej słabości, mojego cierpienia, moich kompleksów i minusów...

Poefizika pozwala mi wznieść się ponad nimi i nad tym wszystkim, nad bytem, nad sposób życia, nad czasem.

Tłumaczył: Grzegorz Kwiatkowski

JĄDRO

Pełzający wieczór – jestem zmęczony od lat
Przenoszę jęk-spojrzenie z tapety na wieniec
Minionych lat –marzenie moje rozpadło się
Pradawnym jadrem od próżnych własnych kłótni.

Wydarzeń brak –
            przenoszę więc pokusy na ich mogiły: ręce –
We krwi, dusza – szlocha gwałtownie.
Kartkuję noc – już brak różnych stronic
Została tylko garść – pożądanych martwych zawstydzeń.

Zasnął poza snem, utuczony sukcesem
Łamiąc prognozy
Wspomnieniem straconych dni:
Lot zastygł w najwyższym punkcie – śmiechem
Nad dawnym pseudosensem
Aby upaść – boleśniej

Tłumaczył: Marian Jaskula

PASAŻER

Jestem po prostu śmiesznym pasażerem
Pociągu do nikąd –
Wyczerpały bezowocne poszukiwania
stacyjki zimnych kwater.

Zapomniany, szary zatroskany
Nie zagrzeję oddechem okna.
Nudnemu, zmęczonemu poboczu,
Brak końca – dno nieuchronności.

śpi ziemia – cierpliwy cmentarz
Grożąc toporami-krzyżami
Duszące łapy "radości"
Kruszą duszę w daremnym wołaniu.

Wiatrowi zostały chwile nadziei
Już nikomu nie ma pieścić bólu,
A w oczach jak za białymi okiennicami,
Beznadziejna tęsknota życia.

Tłumaczył: Marian Jaskula

SITO

Przeglądając strony rozwalonych ulic
Pokręconych ciał obcych miast
Pytałem cień, co nad nim się kłębi,
Skąd przychodzi rozstrzał marzeń.

Zapluty sens przerywa spotkanie
Z ciosem nędzarzy i biczem bogów
Dlatego przelot – sito rozłąki
Przesieje resztę niedorzecznych słów.

Wygładzę wzór przemiany w czułość
Utartymi, wyświechtanymi gestami
          wymyślnych fantazyjnych dni,
Których dawno nie karmi niedbalstwo
               pustych niby-tekstów,
Że śmierci gorzej.

Tłumaczył: Marian Jaskula

www.ingramcontent.com/pod-product-compliance
Lightning Source LLC
Chambersburg PA
CBHW020852090426
42736CB00008B/339